ATLANTIC SALMON

ATLANTIC SALMON

An Illustrated History

ANDREW BARBOUR

CANONGATE PRESS

First published in Great Britain in 1992 by
Canongate Press Plc
14 Frederick Street
Edinburgh EH2 2HB

The publishers gratefully acknowledge copyright permission
granted by the following sources for the right
to reproduce photographs in *Atlantic Salmon*:
Perth Museum and Art Gallery p64 *top, lower left*
His Grace the Duke of Atholl p64 *lower right*
Bill Cowie p11, p59
Niall Campbell p41
Dr Alistair Stephen p60, p69
Havard Groertveldt p78

ISBN 0 86241 372 9

British Library Cataloguing-in-Publication Data
A catalogue record for this book is available on request
from the British Library.

Design by Wide Art, Edinburgh
Printed and bound in Great Britain by
The Bath Press Colour Books,
Blantyre

Contents

Acknowledgements

I would like to thank the following for their help and encouragement in preparing this work: Seonag MacDonald, Robin and Margaret Barbour, Fiona Mackenzie King (Pigeon Press), Niall Campbell, Bill Cowie, Dr Ronald Campbell (Tweed Foundation), Dr Alastair Stephen (West Galloway Fisheries Trust), Janet Stephen and Havard Groentvedt.

Introducing an Extraordinary Fish

It is probably the best-known type of fish in the Northern Hemisphere. It swims, jumps, rolls, dives, leaps, fights, and is even said to 'run'. The salmon, whether the Atlantic or the related Pacific variety, is truly an exceptional fish. Like most precious natural resources, it has been cared for, used, abused, and mismanaged to varying degrees for centuries. The Atlantic salmon in particular is the subject of long-standing political and scientific discussion, not to say argument. Though there have been rapid advances in our knowledge of the fish over the last few decades, each new discovery only unearths another set of demanding questions, making this fish one of the most fascinating of animals.

ATLANTIC ATTRACTION

The Atlantic salmon has been part of our consciousness and culture since time immemorial. This fish has always had a strong symbolism for the peoples who live around the North Atlantic coastlines, from Connecticut to Ungava Bay in the west and from Russia to Spain in the east. In American Indian folklore and Celtic legends the salmon is a sign of the abundance of nature and the seasonality of life. The salmon appears unmistakably in French and Spanish cave art, dating back some 25,000 years, and, further north and many centuries later, on Scots-Pictish symbol stones.

And why not? The small head, the beautifully proportioned and powerful body, the metallic blue-black back, brilliant silver flanks, and pure white belly of the fish fresh from the sea assure the attention of any man, whether he lives in a cave or in a mansion. And the attraction does not end with the aesthetic qualities of the fish. Salmon is food fit for all standards of cuisine, while getting it out of the river and onto a plate, preferably in the most difficult way conceivable – by rod and line – is the ambition of most anglers. Yet despite this avid interest, most people's knowledge of the salmon is shaky to say the least, a situation not helped by the astonishing frequency with which the fish changes appearance, habitat, and even name.

LIFESTYLES

A potted life history can be quite confusing. Life for the salmon starts in fresh water in a very conventional manner as an egg, which is laid in a redd, hatches as an alevin, becomes first a fry and then a parr. Eventually it will go to sea as a smolt. Between then and its end as a kelt, it can be a grilse, kipper, or baggot – all words used throughout the British Isles to describe what is officially known as *Salmo salar*, the leaper. Such a rich and varied nomenclature is no accident, for in any language the variety of words describing a subject reflects the importance of that subject to its native speakers. Thus Scots Gaelic has innumerable words to describe every type of approaching and falling rain, while Eskimos have much to say about snow. It is scarcely suprising, then, to find that few, if any, animals have so many words to describe the different stages in their life-cycle as the salmon. From redd to kelt, this richness of names reflects both the fish's importance to us over the centuries and also its curious and variable patterns of life.

The Atlantic salmon is technically described as an anadromous fish, that is, one which lays its eggs in fresh water but migrates to sea for its major feeding and growth

IT WAS PLINY THE ELDER WHO, IN THE 1ST CENTURY AD, DESCRIBED THE SALMON AS 'THE LEAPER', GIVING THE FISH ITS SPECIFIC NAME *SALAR* (FROM SALIRE: TO LEAP). HIS SUCCINCT TRIBUTE TO THE FISH — 'THE RIVER SALMON SURPASSETH ALL THE FISHES OF THE SEA' — WAS PROBABLY INSPIRED BY SEEING THE HUGE NUMBERS OF FISH THAT ONCE MIGRATED UP THE RHINE, WHERE HE UNDERWENT HIS MILITARY SERVICE.

A SALMON WAITS IN THE PEAT STAINED WATERS DIRECTLY BELOW A WATERFALL BEFORE COMPLETING THE
MIGRATION THAT MAY HAVE TAKEN IT HALF WAY TO AMERICA AND BACK.

stage. Whereas the related sea (or brown) trout and Arctic charr show great variations
in the degree of this migratory behaviour between and even within different stocks, there
are only a few naturally-occuring stocks of salmon which do not migrate to the sea at
all. These are virtually all isolated land-locked populations, found in both Europe and
North America. However, though almost all salmon stocks show a freshwater-to-sea
migratory pattern, there is great variability in the timing of these movements and this
ensures a colourful and intriguing biology.

As a fry and a parr the salmon can spend from one to seven years in fresh water
and, if male, may mature without going to sea at all. Having migrated to the sea as a smolt,
the fish may spend from one to four years away from the river of its birth. Fish that return
after one year in the sea are popularly known as grilse or, in a more technical phrase,
one-seawinter fish. Those that have spent two or more years at sea are simply called
salmon or multi-seawinter fish. If the grilse or salmon survives the rigours of spawning
it may return to the sea as a kelt and go on to spawn in another year. Though only a few
fish overcome the effort and danger of reproduction to spawn again, most populations
of Atlantic salmon contain some repeat spawners, unlike the Pacific salmon species
where all adults invariably die after spawning. With the variation in the amount of time
spent at sea, the adult returning to the rivers can weigh in at anything from less than three

pounds to over seventy. The chance of 'a big one' is a heady draw to the waters for many anglers.

THE GENTLEMAN

Perhaps what adds the icing to the salmon cake is the long-standing commercial interest in the species. People tend to take a sharper interest in any animal when there is money to be made out of it, and in countries such as Norway or Scotland, where the salmon has always been plentiful, the fish has been an important economic resource for the last eight hundred years or more.

Yet the respect reserved for the fish has more than just the glitter of financial silver behind it. An example of the high esteem, or even awe, in which the salmon has been held in many rural areas can be seen from the fact that the fish is a member of that elite band of characters whose names are banned through superstition from being spoken out loud on-board Scottish fishing boats. The list includes swans and ministers of religion, but whereas the minister is rather irreverently referred to as the 'sky pilot', the salmon has swum under a more distinguished banner, as 'the fish' or 'the gentleman'.

Few folk would disagree that the Atlantic salmon with its beautifully athletic form really is nature's perfect 'gentleman' of the aquatic world.

THE JUVENILE STAGE — THE PARR — JUST BEFORE THE MIGRATION TO THE SEA
AND A NEW LIFE IN THE ATLANTIC.

A European Fish

To study the past and present distribution of the Atlantic salmon through its European waters is to study the industrial and social development of a large chunk of the continent, from Russia down to Portugal and including such unlikely countries as Switzerland and Czechoslovakia; and though the sizes of the populations found today in Europe are a mere fraction of those recorded in medieval times, the salmon still occupies both the Iberian and Kola peninsulas at opposite ends of the continent, with more than just a few rivers in between.

THE IBERIAN PENINSULA

Salmon and eucalyptus trees may seem an unlikely mix of fauna and flora. The north of Portugal and the north-west provinces of Spain, Gallicia, and Asturias grow both and, the cynics would say, treat both with equal disdain. The wooded hills, planted with eucalyptus this century to supply pulp timber, are regularly set alight through the summer months in a deliberate attempt to create grazing, affect the timber market, and generally cause political trouble. The rivers that flow past such scenes of destruction (such as the Rio Tambre in Gallicia) hold good stocks of trout, but salmon are now only occasionally caught. Attempts in the 1980s to stock these rivers with hatchery-reared smolts largely failed, not least because the descending migrants were caught in the rivers and netted out from the sea before they even had a chance to put on some weight. Spain has a problem educating her fish-buying public not to create a market for undersized fish: to the Spanish consumer a smolt is just as good a meal as a sardine, and for the fisherman, professional or otherwise, it is a safer bet than waiting for the returning adult.

Nevertheless, some adult fish do turn up on the west coast of Portugal and Spain, and one, the river Ulla, still holds a regular stock. Historically, the Duoro and the Mino, of which the latter forms the border between Spain and Portugal, held very rich salmon fishings, and these formed the southernmost limit of the salmon's European range.

It is on the north coast of Spain that the Iberian peninsula's better salmon rivers are found today. The short, fast-flowing rivers drain a green and beautiful coastal strip of land, far removed from the Spain of package holidays and frazzled foreigners. The main part of this northern coast has a backbone of mountains and hills, whose rivers are fed by snowmelt in spring and a relatively high rainfall throughout much of the year.

Of the twenty or so Spanish rivers that hold stocks of salmon, only half a dozen return catches of more than a hundred fish a year. The rivers Deva and Cares, which join together some 15 km from the sea, are spectacular examples of these southern European salmon waters. Both rise in the central and highest part of the limestone *massif*, the Picos de Europa, and both have cut immense gorges through classic mountain scenery. High snowfields, giant rock buttresses, forests of chestnut and the evergreen holm oak, all overlook the greenish waters of these two rivers. The colour of the rivers comes from the dissolved salts and minerals leached from the limestone, and in the Deva the levels of copper and zinc are high enough to cause problems for young hatching alevins. Partly for this reason, and also because the Cares has better access to suitable spawning grounds, it is the Cares that has the larger run of

THE RIO CARES

salmon. Currently, two hundred or more fish are landed every year by anglers fishing the better beats, or *cotos* as they are known. These *cotos* on the Deva-Cares, as on the other salmon rivers, are much sought after and hence rather exclusive. They are allocated by ballot, and the successful applicants are carefully watched by bailiffs, or *guardas*, whose duties are to register all fish caught. Though the fishermen may include Spanish and foreign royalty, there are no airs or graces about the methods used to hook a fish – the humble worm is the favoured technique, fished on a huge seven-to-ten metre rod.

Like Iceland, Spain is unusual in allowing no netting for salmon in the sea or estuaries, though the inevitable 'accidental catch' does take place there. This ban, enacted in 1942, is a legacy of General Franco's rule. A keen salmon fisherman, Franco was brought up beside a Gallician salmon stream. It was he who oversaw most of Spain's present salmon legislation, aimed at holding on to the remnants of what was once a huge resource.

SPAIN

Over Franco's lifetime the annual salmon catch in Spain had fallen tenfold to only 2000 to 3000 fish. This drop was mainly due to overfishing, but the real damage had come about through the building of weirs and dams during the preceeding century as industrialisation spread through the country. These dams either lacked salmon ladders or had badly designed ones that even the most athletic fish found impossible to scale. Nothing kills a salmon river faster than erecting a dam which prevents fish from reaching their spawning grounds. Pollution and overfishing can decimate a stock, but the wholesale destruction of salmon rivers throughout Europe has its roots in the dams and weirs which powered the mills of the Industrial Revolution. The Deva and Cares escaped the damming of their waters and owe their present stocks to this.

FRANCE

Further east along the coast and across the border into France, the rivers of the western Pyrenees have also retained small salmon populations. With the exception of the Nivelle, all are tributaries of the Adour which empties its waters into the Bay of Biscay by Bayonne and Biarritz. There are the remnants of a commercial net fishery in the much polluted Adour estuary and coastal waters, the annual catch of which has dwindled from 10,000 some fifty years ago to no more than a few hundred today.

Rising in Spain, but running mainly through France, the Nivelle has a small salmon population which has been carefully nurtured by biologists at the Government's research centre at St Pée. This delightful stream flows through hilly limestone countryside and is fed by underground springs that help to keep the water cool through the summer. An electronic fish counter and smolt trap give details of the salmon population, and this stock, which usually numbers 300 spawning adults each year, is characteristic of these southern waters. The first arrivals are normally in mid April and consist of fish of three to four kilograms. Forming the major part of the population, they have gone to sea as one or two-year-old smolts.

Further up the west coast of France, the Loire is the next river where today's angler can still see salmon. Only one tributary of this heavily industrialised river – the Allier – holds a spawning stock. Salmon here have one of the longest journeys in Europe to reach their spawning grounds in the centre of France, a distance of just under 800 km. The population consists of fish

THE CANALISED RIVER AULNE IN BRITTANY HAS SALMON LADDERS ON EACH LOCK GATE. AN ANGLER TRIES HIS LUCK IN THESE TAMED WATERS.

FRANCE

which, having spent two or more years at sea, return early in the year to the French coast in time to reach their destination in the Allier headwaters before summer water levels drop and temperatures soar in the river and conditions are not conducive to successful salmon migration.

The best chance of seeing a French salmon lies in the streams of Brittany and Normandy. A high rainfall over the granite hills of the Armorican plateau and the Normandy fields supplies the water for a total of twenty-one salmon rivers, such as the Aulne, the Blavet, and the Elorn. The latter flows into the Rade de Brest in North Finistere and is held up as a model of river management. Only 42 km long, somewhere between 100 and 300 salmon are landed on rod and line from the Elorn every year – 10% of the Breton catch and 5% of the French total. Yet this is a river which at the turn of the century was dead, with 180 tanneries and 140 other mills damming and polluting the waters. In 1969, however, with much of this rural industry dead and gone, it was decided to try to reinstate salmon to this small stream. With much hard work and the help of a hatchery producing 10,000 smolts a year, the 1980s have seen a welcome return of this prized French fish. France has plenty of other rivers which once held salmon and now beg to be given the same chance as the Elorn. The country is lucky to have had the Breton and Pyrenean streams which, because of their geographical isolation, retained a fraction of France's historically-recorded salmon wealth.

SALMON CAUGHT BY CONTROVERSIAL MONOFILAMENT DRIFTNETS SEVERAL MILES OFF THE NE ENGLISH COAST – NETS THAT ARE BANNED BY LAW IN THE NEIGHBOURING SCOTTISH WATERS. THIS FISHERMAN LANDS HIS CATCH AT NORTH SHIELDS.

THE LOW COUNTRIES

Germany, Holland, Belgium, and Czechoslovakia have nothing left of their salmon resources, whilst Poland only retains a token salmon population in one river. The Rhine, the Meuse, the Seine, the Elbe, and the Oder – the great rivers that drain so much of western Europe – were once the richest salmon-producing rivers the continent could boast of. But salmon in these waters were casualties of the Industrial Revolution. The fate of the Rhine is one of Europe's sadder ecological tales.

The Rhine, 1320 km long, had a unique stock of salmon that spawned in the tributaries downstream of the Rheinfall at Schaffhausen. Switzerland, France, Germany, and Holland all shared this rich resource, netting salmon in their thousands right up to Goarhausen, home of the

Lorelei, some 400 kilometres from the North Sea. The Dutch estuary nets
alone took 69,000 fish in the 1885 season, averaging 8 kg each, but by 1907
the catch for the entire river had dropped to 65,000 and by the 1950s the
Rhine salmon was extinct. Again, it was the erection of dams, weirs, and
locks, aided by a disgraceful pollution record, which did the damage. In the
days before European Community co-operation, the international nature of
the river was a definite hindrance to rescue plans. Nowadays one of the few
places to see a salmon on the Rhine is in Koblenz's Middle Rhine Museum – a sad end
to the salmon in Europe's best-known northern river.

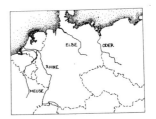

THE LOW COUNTRIES

E N G L A N D   A N D   W A L E S

Across the Channel, England's larger salmon rivers shared a fate similar to that of
the Rhine. Having lost its salmon last century, the Thames is not often thought of
as a salmon river by Londoners. Yet strenuous efforts have been made by the
former Water Authority to persuade the fish to return, through extensive stocking of
imported eggs and fry, and now one hundred or more adult fish make their way past
the Houses of Parliament every year. None the less, London sees more salmon than most
cities through its Billingsgate market, which handles a significant part of the wild salmon
catch of the United Kingdom.

For statistical purposes, Wales gets lumped in with England for most things,
including salmon catches. The principality is actually responsible for about 40% of the
combined English and Welsh rod catch. The River Wye, shared jointly by both countries
but drawing most of its water from Wales, is perhaps the best salmon river in this part
of the kingdom. With about 5000 fish a year on rod and line, the river is responsible for
25% of the sporting catch in England and Wales. This is not bad for a river whose total
catch was reduced to fewer than 500 at the turn of the century as a result of an overzealous
netting industry. From 1862 to 1904 the local landowners, under the auspices
of the Wye Preservation Society, bought out netting rights on the river, and the
last large-scale netting ceased in the 1920s. Angling on the Wye has vied not
only with netting, but also more recently with forestry. A potential clash of
interests between commercial forestry and freshwater fisheries may be
suprising to many people, but the planned afforestation of much of the Wye's
catchment areas was resisted – successfully – by the former Welsh Water
Authority on the grounds of the adverse hydrological effects of commercial
forestry operations.

ENGLAND AND WALES

Though the Wye river nets have been largely bought off, most English
and Welsh rivers, including the Wye, do have netting activities in their

17

THE RIVER TAY HAS A HUGE CATCHMENT AREA: HERE THE CARCASS OF A KELT ROTS ON THE BANK OF ONE OF THE TAY'S TRIBUTARIES, THE TUMMEL. SUCH FISH WILL PROVIDE AN EASY MEAL FOR OTTERS, MINK AND FOXES.

estuaries. Drift nets are found in the Dee and Usk estuaries and further north in the Ribble on the Lancashire coast. However, much of this has a traditional flavour, with the use of coracles for instance, though the nets are as modern as they come. This part of the industry on the west and south coasts of Britain lands as many salmon as the rods do, with an annual catch of between 20,000 and 30,000 fish during the eighties.

The major English netting industry, however, is sited off the north-east coast of England. Working out of harbours such as North Shields on the Tyne, small boats have fished drift nets for over a hundred years. Modern monofilament materials, introduced in the 1960s, have improved the efficiency of these gill nets – 'curtains of death', as their detractors call them. The boats operate during daylight hours through the summer months and through the 1980s boosted the total annual salmon catch for England and Wales to between 70,000 and 100,000 fish. This is a controversial fishery, much criticised by fishermen in Scotland, as most of the fish caught are destined for Scottish rivers from the Tweed north to the Esk. In 1991 the British government finally bowed to pressure and announced the gradual phasing out of this drift netting. Undoubtedly, the fishery's presence has weakened the arguments of those in the United Kingdom who call for an end to the high-seas fisheries off the Faroes and Greenland.

SCOTLAND

A similar industry started to develop off the north-east coast of Scotland in the late 1960s but was quickly banned when public concern mounted over the effect on stocks. Scotland has fared better in retaining her salmon populations than many other European countries but, like Norway, Iceland, and Russia, this has been due largely to accidents of geography and history. A lower level of industrialisation, aided by a small, scattered human population, left the bulk of Scottish rivers in a relatively pristine condition. The Industrial Revolution in England had destroyed much of that country's salmon stocks, so it is ironic that the wealth created by this development of English industry should have helped to preserve the stocks of Scotland and Norway. As industrialists and aristocrats began to recognise and value the sporting potential of rivers in these remote countries, so they used their money to purchase fishing rights and hence protect stocks.

Scottish rivers such as the Tay, the Tweed, and the Spey, are among Europe's best today. The biggest river in the United Kingdom, the Tay has had annual catches of between 29,000 and 105,000 over the last twenty-five years, mostly taken by the various netting stations in the tidal waters. Unlike the shorter rivers on the Scottish west coast, a large proportion of the Tay's fish are multi-seawinter, and it is these that are the chief prey of the angler. However, through the 1980s grilse outnumbered the multi-seawinter salmon in the river's netting catches. This may be changing: in the first two years of the 1990s there has been a poor run of grilse, arriving late in September just before the netting stations have to shut down. As in many other rivers, attempts have been made by angling interests to buy out these estuary nets; however, in this case the price tag of £1,000,000 has proved too high for the bid to be successful.

SCOTLAND

I R E L A N D

Scotland feels that she fares badly through other countries' netting activities. On the west coast, for instance, many of the fish returning to the short-spate rivers are escapees from the Irish drift net fishery off the Donegal coast. Ireland is a major salmon-producing nation, though only a small fraction of the 1000 to 2000 tonnes of wild salmon landed in the country is caught on rod and line. There has long been a netting industry, based on the seine and drift nets. Drift netting in the open sea expanded rapidly in the 1960s with the development of modern gill nets. This latter activity is heavily criticised as being quite out of control, with regulations flouted as to net length, number of operating boats, and areas fished. Being sensitive to such accusations, new fishery protection boats were introduced by the Navy and the Regional Fishery Boards in 1989 to police the drift netters. The decline in reported catches in the early 1990s in these Irish waters has been attributed in part to the efforts of these boats, as well as to an apparent drop in the numbers of salmon available to be caught.

Though probably better known for its trout fishing, Ireland has some superb salmon rivers. The Blackwater and the Moy are great angling rivers but, like the Nivelle in France, it is in some of the smaller river systems that the research effort has been concentrated. The Burrishoole fishery in County Mayo has been run by the Salmon Research Trust of Ireland since 1957, while the River Bush in Northern Ireland, as well as providing water for a famous whiskey, has provided data on salmon stocks for the Department of Agriculture since 1973. Both river systems have been important in developing an understanding of salmon stock recruitment and management.

IRELAND

The sun sets on an Icelandic river north of Reykyavik. Anglers in Iceland are not allowed to make use of the long daylight hours in summer: fishing is restricted to between the hours of 7am and 10pm.

I C E L A N D

While the British Isles lie square in the middle of the salmon's European freshwater range, the north-eastern corner is taken up by Iceland. This remote part of Europe has protected its salmon resource with the single-mindedness that is possible when there is a small, homogenous population who understand the value of fishery conservation. In 1932 all sea fishing for salmon ended in Icelandic waters, and though there is a vestige of netting in

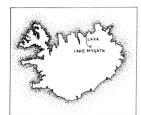

ICELAND

three glacial rivers in the south and west, Iceland has devoted her salmon to the angler. About eighty rivers yield some 50,000 fish a year, and with the financial benefits brought by foreign anglers going directly to the local communities on the rivers, few would disagree that Iceland has a sound, sustainable salmon management policy.

The importance of salmon to Iceland in the past is easily appreciated when one realises how many of her rivers are named 'Laxa', the Scandinavian name for the fish. One of these, the Laxa in Adaldalur in the north-east of the country, flows out of the extraordinary Lake Myvatn. Set amidst fantastic volcanic scenery, the contrast with the salmon rivers of Spain, England, or Russia could not be greater.

N O R W A Y

While salmon in Iceland are mainly one-seawinter fish, and large fish are unusual, the same could not be said for certain rivers in Norway, the Scandinavian country best known for its salmon waters. In 1989 Norway joined Iceland in banning netting in its coastal waters, though sea nets are still fished in Finnmark in the very north of the country, well inside the Arctic Circle. Most of Norway's 400 or so salmon rivers are short, crashing their way down her spectacular mountain scenery over impassable waterfalls. The rivers of Finnmark are different in character, however, and in the Tana and the Alta Norway has two of the world's most remarkable salmon rivers. The Alta is famed for its large salmon, whilst the Tana is known for the sheer numbers of fish landed each year.

The River Alta, which enters Norway through the birch-covered Finnmark plateau as the Kautokeino, is a river rich in Arctic grayling and charr. Salmon swim only in the lower 45 km of the river, which is called the Altaelva by the locals. The gorge at the top of the huge Savco Canyon with its impassable falls stops any migrant fish, though a few kilometres further upstream the controversial Planlagtdemning hydroelectrical complex leaves the river bed in the gorge dry in low flow conditions. The Alta fishing season starts on the first of June, and with twenty-four hours of daylight the first fish of the season is sometimes caught on the stroke of midnight. The initial three weeks of the

SCANDINAVIA AND RUSSIA

21

season are open to all locals who can claim to be farmers – possession of a cow allows you to fish one of the most exclusive waters in the world! – but after that it is a different story. A local committee handles bids for the different beats on the river and distributes the income among the farmers. The river attracts some of the world's richest anglers and, with considerable numbers of fish each weighing over 20 kg landed some years, the prizes are indeed large. Between 1400 and 3000 fish are landed every year on rod and

SALMON IN THE RIVER ALTA IN FINNMARK WERE CAUGHT BY CRUIVE AND TRAP FISHERIES, INITIATED BY THE RUSSIANS IN THE 17TH CENTURY, BUT CONTROLLED BY COMMERCIAL INTERESTS IN BERGEN OR COPENHAGEN, UNTIL THE BRITISH ARRIVED IN THE MID-19TH CENTURY WITH THEIR RODS AND THEIR MONEY. SINCE THEN THE RIVER HAS BECOME FAMED FOR ITS FINE SPORT WITH LARGE FISH.

line on the Alta, with an overall average weight of seven to nine kilograms during the 1980s. This places the Alta in the top five salmon rivers in Norway, though a long way behind the Tana with its annual catch of between 10,000 and 20,000 fish.

R U S S I A

East of the Tana lie perhaps the most unspoilt salmon rivers in the world. Banned to all but the Red Army until recently, the rivers and streams in the 'no-go' Soviet area of the Norwegian-Russian border were a complete unknown, even to Soviet biologists. The latter have been allowed to visit some of these rivers, as the Cold War paranoia and the centralised authority of the Soviet Union disintegrates. The Russian rivers entering into the White Sea and the Barents Sea are as rich in their salmon resource as any in Norway, Scotland, or Iceland, but rather less well-publicised. The Kola peninsula alone has sixty-five salmon-producing rivers, and the strict management of this resource is in contrast to the situation in western Europe. No sea netting is allowed on this coast, and fish in each major river are exploited on a stock-by-stock basis – a desirable

A SALMON TRAP SITS BESIDE THE TULOMA RIVER, NEAR MURMANSK. IN POST SOVIET RUSSIA, HOW WILL THESE RICH SALMON POPULATIONS BE EXPLOITED?

feature of any rational management plan for salmon populations. However, sport angling has been discouraged and is only allowed on smaller rivers that are not commercially fished. The major rivers have netting stations above tidal waters which allow complete interception of all the migrating fish. The nets, consisting of a fence and trap, are fished on alternate days to allow a calculated escapement. Only one river in the former Soviet Union – the Kolbitsa – was open to foreign anglers during the 1980s. In 1991 the pressing need for foreign cash meant that access to several other rivers began to be granted to visiting sportsmen with enough money to buy a Russian adventure.

The Varsuga river on the Kola peninsula is now one of Russia's most productive rivers, with a catch of 20,000 to 50,000 fish a year. Though well inside the Arctic Circle, the rivers of this region are warm in summer, occasionally reaching up to 19° C, and growth of the young parr is suprisingly fast. The Varsuga even has a proportion of two-year-old smolts, but most rivers in this region produce three to four-year-old smolts, which return from their feeding grounds in the Barents Sea as three to four-kilogram fish the following summer. June to August are the usual months for fish to run in all the northern rivers of the Kola peninsula. The Varsuga and other rivers flowing into the White Sea also have a substantial autumn run of salmon, and the Varsuga in particular is unique

DANISH DRIFT NETTERS, WITH THE FLAGGED BOUYS OR 'DANS', AWAIT IN BORNHOLM FOR THE AUTUMN SALMON
SEASON TO START.

in many ways, not least by producing very small, young smolts which return as very small grilse.

The White Sea with its surrounding pine and spruce forests was for a long time the centre of Russian civilisation. Until the sixteenth century, north-flowing rivers, such as the Dvina or Onega, provided the Russians with their main means of communication with western Europe before the Baltic trade routes developed. These rivers also produced great salmon fishings, which, with the threat of overexploitation, have just recently been closed.

Further east, the Pechora is Russia's longest salmon river. Since 1988 the net fishery has been closed as a precautionary move to protect the numerous stocks on this huge waterway. The Pechora, which carries water from the western Urals some 1760 km past the sites of Stalin's infamous camps, had a huge netting industry at its mouth. With stake nets stretching a kilometre right across the river, all migrating fish were caught every second day from early summer until November. The Pechora is the most easterly salmon river of note in Russia, though a warming of sea temperatures has led to some fish entering rivers flowing into the Kara Sea. The limits of sea ice effectively determine the geographical range of the fish in this part of the world.

T H E B A L T I C C O U N T R I E S

These Arctic rivers are not the only salmon waters in European Russia. The Baltic side of the country has its own salmon waters which, like Sweden's and Finland's, contribute to the isolated stocks of salmon in the Baltic. Though the same species as the Atlantic salmon, the stocks of the Baltic fish are largely separated from their better-known brethren in the Atlantic and are biologically quite distinct.

The Baltic salmon tend to be small in size, and most stay in the brackish waters of this sea for only a year before returning to their native rivers. In the Gulf of Finland, stocks of salmon from the Russian, Estonian, and Finnish streams scarcely migrate from their home coast, feeding on the local population of spratts. A Russian fishing fleet makes good use of this stock, while the rest of the Baltic fishery is shared among Swedish, Finnish, and Danish boats, the latter operating from the island of Bornholm in the southern Baltic.

Bornholm has long been a centre for salmon fishing boats. Today, the Danish boats are limited to a small part of the southern Baltic, but about forty boats still make a living from summer fishing for cod and winter fishing for salmon. About 1000 tonnes of salmon are still landed from September to June each year in ports such as Nexo, by both Danish and some Polish vessels working the multifilament drift nets to the east of the island.

Sweden and Finland may not be renowned for their salmon fishings, but the two countries are the champions of stocking and release of hatchery-reared smolts to compensate for lost wild stocks. Both countries lost the bulk of their many salmon rivers through the first fifty years of this century. Damming for hydroelectric and other purposes and destruction of spawning habitat by the timber industry, together with basic, old-fashioned industrial and domestic pollution, left both these Scandinavian countries with a fraction of their former salmon resource. The solution, developed since the turn of the century but given special impetus after the Second World War, was to compensate for the loss of river habitat by releasing hatchery-reared smolts near the sea. The results have justified the effort, and by the early 70s the Swedish annual releases of over 2,000,000 smolts were responsible alone for two thirds of the total salmon stock in the Baltic. Many of the hatchery techniques subsequently used by the salmon-farming industry in the 1970s were pioneered in Finland and Sweden.

The main salmon-producing waters for both countries are now in the Gulf of Bothnia, near their joint border. But both countries, along with Russia and Norway, have stocks of land-locked salmon, notably in Lake Vannern in Sweden and in Lake Iso-Saimaa in Finland. Both lakes, in addition to Lake Ladoga near St Petersburg, supported commercial fisheries, but the fate of these lakes has been no better than that of the rivers of their neighbouring countries, through the effects of hydroelectric schemes and pollution. The Russian land-locked stocks in Lake Ladoga, though they never reach the sea, can still produce specimens of over 10 kg in size. But the land-locked stocks elsewhere, such as in Norway's River Namsen, tend to be dwarf versions of their ocean-going colleagues, stunted by a lack of the rich feeding that can be found at sea.

A EUROPEAN CHALLENGE

It may suprise some people that salmon can be found from the Baltic to the Bay of Biscay. Yet, the fish's spawning requirement for cool, clean, fast-flowing waters could be met by most European countries. How shameful it is that access to many of these spawning grounds has been denied to the salmon as a result of decades of European indifference to the needs of the fish. We can only hope that less apathy in the years to come will bring countries like Spain and France into the same league as Norway, Scotland, Iceland, and Ireland, as top wild salmon producers on the eastern side of the Atlantic.

Fresh Water

It may seem curious that the rich orange-coloured egg, the start of a salmon's life, is laid in its gravel nest or 'redd' in the late autumn and early winter months when life round about seems to be going into cold storage. But, like the oak tree's acorn, it is all a question of timing. By the time the pace of life picks up in the spring, the salmon egg has hatched and the young fry is ready to make best use of the coming season of plenty. Lying deep in the gravel bed of the streams and rivers where the mother or 'hen' fish had excavated her redd, kept safe from the overlying ice, the egg has slowly been developing at a tempo determined by the temperature of its surroundings.

THE EGG

The eggs are rich in yolk and large in comparison with those of many other fish species, with a diameter of about half a centimetre. The deep golden or red colour comes from the carotenoid pigments, the same type of pigment that gives peppers or tomatoes their rich colour. Such pigments have an anti-oxidant role among other functions. There is no hard outer shell but rather an elastic membrane which gives the egg great strength, able to resist the weight of any overlying stones.

The embryo develops slowly, and half–way through hatching the eyes and the shape of the head can be seen clearly. Up to this point, the egg is rather sensitive to disturbance but once 'eyed', as fish farmers and bailiffs call this stage, the eggs can be moved with ease. Temperature is the most important factor affecting how long it will take the egg to hatch. At a steady 8° C an egg will hatch after eight weeks, whereas at 1° C the same egg will require about thirty weeks' incubation. Temperatures above 12° C seem to cause developmental abnormalities in the embryos, and this is an important limiting factor determining the geographical range of the fish.

THE ALEVIN

At hatching, the embryo or 'alevin' splits its egg case with the aid of special hatching enzymes. It is then able to stretch out to its full length, a shade under 2 cm from nose to tail. It is still lying in its gravel home, and here it will stay until the yolk sac is nearly all used up. Through this period the alevin instinctively reacts in order to stay in

NEWLY STRIPPED SALMON EGGS, PRIOR TO FERTILISATION, HAVE YET TO ABSORB WATER AND SO TO SWELL TO THEIR NORMAL SPHERICAL SHAPE — A PHENOMENON KNOWN AS WATER HARDENING.

its dark surroundings, and if disturbed it will try to escape the light. Otherwise it will lie still, a light grey body with a bulbous orange ball of yolk attached to its gut like some strange growth; but it is the alevin that is growing while its yolk reserves shrink, and after about forty days following hatching in the cold spring temperatures of northern Europe, the alevin is ready to start looking for new sources of food.

THE   FRY

With about 90% of their original yolk gone, the alevins become 'fry' and suddenly find a liking for light and the outside world. The fry start emerging from the gravel beds in April in southern waters and through to June in the more northerly latitudes, and eventually will disperse from the redd.

These changes in behaviour ensure that the alevin remained safe deep in the gravel while it used up its yolk; yet at the right time it is ready to move to the surface of the stream bed then to disperse to utilise whatever suitable habitat it may chance upon. These instincts and the forces which control the changes are a mystery. One day they may be determined, but this need never stop us from admiring the efficiency and beauty of such behaviour patterns.

THE   PARR

After it disperses from the redd and once it gains distinctive grey markings on its flanks, the fry is called a 'parr' for the major part of its first freshwater residence. Few animals are honoured by so many changes of name! The parr now faces the normal problems of animal life in the wild – to eat and not be eaten. The aquatic larvae of mayflies, stoneflies, and chironomid midges will probably make up the bulk of the parr's prey. The young fish will take up and defend a territory against others of its own age, and will quickly find one or more favourite feeding stations. Brothers, sisters, and strangers alike are all rivals, and no favours are given. The ranges or territories of different fish may overlap, depending on the density of fish in a stream, but they will probably form a dominance heirarchy, as studies on fish in tanks have clearly shown.

Parr that do not find a suitable territory quickly will have to move further up or downstream or else take up a less than perfect patch. Those fish which would be surplus to the stream's maximum population-carrying capacity are most likely to perish through starvation or predation. The parr that does set up a territory will lie facing upstream on or just above the river bed, from where it will dart out to grab an unlucky nymph or spent fly that might drift past on the current. One study in a Highland stream in Scotland showed that most feeding depends on such drifting invertebrates, with only about a quarter of the feeding effort devoted to finding prey on the gravel itself. Feeding behaviour may vary from river to river. Parr in the huge Pechora river in Russia, for instance, are thought to feed mainly on animals living on the river bottom. However, it is generally considered that the bulk of the prey for most populations of parr is carried on the current.

Relying on drifting insects might seem a rather chancy diet, but, for reasons only partially guessed at, a large number of aquatic insect larvae do leave the stones where they normally hide to take a ride on the current every now and again. And furthermore, there is a daily rhythm to this 'invertebrate drift', and the parr lies ready to intercept. Sometimes the joy-riding insect larvae is well studied by the fish, which drifts downstream before making a grab and then quickly returning to its lookout point on the river bed. Many of the insects floating past the fish in the current may have fallen into the water from overhanging vegetation, and in smaller streams this source of food can be quite important to the parr. Maintaining bankside vegetation is vital, therefore, for providing both food and cover for young salmonids.

Not surprisingly, certain parts of a river will produce more drifting insects than others. The fast-flowing, shallow waters, known as 'riffles', tend to be

THE ALEVIN IS REALLY AN EMBRYONIC STAGE, DEPENDENT ON ITS YOLK RESERVES TO SUSTAIN IT THROUGH ITS DEVELOPMENT.

29

DEPENDENT ON SIGHT TO CAPTURE FOOD, THE FRY KEEP A LOOKOUT FOR A SUITABLE DISH. ON APPEARING FROM THE REDD, THE FRY MAY DISPERSE UP TO 100M UPSTREAM AND FURTHER DOWNSTREAM IN THE QUEST FOR A SUITABLE HABITAT.

better in this respect than the deeper pools, and so the proportion of different habitats in a section of stream or river will determine to some degree the size of population it can hold. Other factors come into play here, such as the ubiquitous temperature consideration and the total invertebrate productivity of an area, i.e. the amount of food available, but the water depth does seem to be important, with parr in their first year preferring the riffle type of habitat. Variations in habitat suitability mean that a ten-yard stretch of a narrow stream may hold anything from one to ten suitable parr territories. Yet this stretch of stream would, on average, produce fewer than one fish ready to migrate to the sea.

As the fish grows it may require a larger territory to satisfy its food needs, and it may shift to deeper water, again depending on the characteristics of the stream in question. Some studies have shown that the parr are very faithful to their territories, and will live out their entire freshwater life in the same well-defined home range, provided that the habitat is suitable. Fish that have had to move, through competition from a more aggressive fish or loss of habitat during a drought or following a spate, will probably be displaced downstream, and hence may become very susceptible to predation in their homeless state. However, little is known of what befalls a fish under these circumstances and scientists are now very interested in the fate of such fish — do predators select them in preference to fitter ones or do subordinate and displaced fish simply starve?

GROWTH RATES

The migration of the parr to the sea – when it is known as a 'smolt' – always takes place in late spring or early summer. How long the parr has stayed in the river before this migration depends on its rate of growth, and so ultimately on temperature and food availability. In most parts of the British Isles and in much of Scandinavia and Russia, most parr will make the move to the sea after two to four years in the river, but in waters partially fed by glaciers in Norway and Iceland, parr may be seven or eight years old before they make the change. By contrast, some parr will move to sea after only one year in the rich, warmer waters of southern England, France, or Spain. The reason for this dependence on growth rate is that there seems to be a minimum size – of about 12 to 13 cm – below which the fish is unable to make the transition to the sea. In the colder waters of the fish's range, parr may be growing at less than 2 cm per year because of the low temperatures and low food productivity of the streams, while in the warmer, richer southern waters, a parr can make the smolting size within one year. As usual with any biological rule, there are exceptions, and in the Kola peninsula in Russia the stocks of salmon in the Varsuga river migrate to sea at half this minimum size, as two-year-old fish. However, these fish stay within the low-salinity waters of the White Sea until the autumn, when they are at a size to survive the full-strength sea water of the Barents Sea.

THE SALMON PARR CAN BE CONFUSED WITH A YOUNG BROWN TROUT, BUT IT LACKS THE RED ADIPOSE FIN OF THE YOUNG TROUT, AND HAS 10–12 'THUMBPRINT' MARKS COMPARED TO THE TROUT'S 9–10. THE SALMON PARR ALSO HAS A SHORTER 'TOP-LIP' (*MAXILLA*) WHICH DOES NOT EXTEND PAST THE EYE, IN CONTRAST TO THAT OF THE TROUT.

The growth rates of parr have been studied under controlled conditions by biologists on both sides of the Atlantic and have shown some curious characteristics. In a population of parr that might be expected to migrate to sea in the following year, two groups of fish can be identified in the autumn months preceeding the spring migration. One is a fast-growing group which keeps on feeding, if possible, through the winter and will migrate in the spring. The other is a slow-growing group whose development is retarded and which will spend a further year in the river as parr before migrating seawards. Parr in this latter group actually show a repressed appetite and appear to have made a 'decision' to hold themselves back in their development. It seems that this physiological decision to grow up and go to sea, or to hold back and stay at home, is taken in July and August in the year preceeding migration, but it is only by the autumn that the growth difference can be spotted. The decision is influenced by food availability and growth rate during this critical summer 'time window', which then affects behaviour a whole year later. The notion of a fish making a decision may seem ludicrous, but in effect that is just what happens.

THE MATURE PARR

Though considered juveniles, many of the male parr, though not the females, may in fact mature before they ever reach the sea, forming an extra, uninvited breeding

31

THREE GENERATIONS OF PARR — GROWTH RATES MAY BE SLOW IN THE COLD WATERS OF MORE NORTHERLY RIVERS, CONDITIONS THAT SEEM TO FAVOUR THE PRODUCTION OF FISH THAT ONE DAY WILL RETURN AS LARGE MULTI-SEAWINTER SALMON (THOUGH NO ONE KNOWS WHY).

partner with two full-sized 'adult' fish. This adds a further complication to our understanding of the parr's decision-making. Such sexual precocity can affect up to 100% of the male parr in a population. Many of these fish will never reach the sea, either suffering in the heavy mortalities associated with spawning, or else remaining in the rivers for further years. However, some of these parr are found migrating to sea in the spring following maturation. Biologists believe that these two facets of parr life, maturation and migration to the sea, are physiologically conflicting and that one precludes the other. However, a very few fish will mature in their first summer at sea as smolts; they are sometimes referred to as 'pre-grilse' or 'Jack' salmon, the latter term also being used for mature parr.

The sexually-precocious parr will mate successfully with adult females, and can be present in large numbers on the spawning beds. They certainly form an extra partner with two conventional adult fish, but it is doubtful whether they will attract females to spawn by themselves without the presence of a full-sized, 'sea-run' male. The ripe male parr may be adopting a rather sneaky reproductive strategy here, fertilising eggs where the hard work has already been done by another fish. Many parr have another interest in mind at this time – their bellies. Loose eggs drifting downstream are quickly snapped up as a nutritious meal and, not surprisingly, the full-grown male will do his utmost to keep these unscrupulous juveniles at bay, turning and snapping with his huge jaws.

Why does the female parr not also mature? For her, the number of eggs she could produce is tiny compared with a sea-run adult, and so it is not worth while if, as is normal, she can gain access to the sea.

T H E   S M O L T

The ripe male parr will be found migrating through river systems in the autumn, but the main parr movements are in the spring, when they undergo the internal and external modifications necessary for a life at sea, a process known as 'smolting'. While the parr is ideally suited to a life in fast-flowing waters – its pectoral fins acting like hydroplanes to keep the fish on the river bottom with the minimum of effort – the new smolt is an animal adapted for life in the open sea. Unwilling to swim against fast currents, and rapidly developing a silver colouration in its scales and skin, the smolt drifts and swims downstream in an unhurried fashion, choosing the cover of darkness as its favoured time of travel. Leaving its home territory in March and April, or even earlier in some of the upland headwaters of a river, it may find itself in the estuary by May or June. By then it is perfectly prepared for a sea life, and accordingly rather poorly suited to remaining in the rivers. Smolts in Arctic rivers migrate rather later in the year, in June or

A FLASH OF SILVER AS THE SMOLT MIGRATES TOWARDS THE SEA. MOVING AT NIGHT, THE SMOLT IS LESS WILLING TO SWIM AGAINST FAST CURRENTS THAN THE PARR, AND MAY BE INADVERTENTLY CARRIED DOWNSTREAM TOWARDS THE ESTUARY.

A BIOLOGIST ELECTROFISHES A HILL STREAM TO GAIN AN ESTIMATE OF THE SALMONID POPULATION DENSITY. A PULSED CURRENT IS PASSED BETWEEN TWO ELECTRODES PLACED IN THE WATER. FISH ARE AFFECTED BY THE ELECTRICAL FIELD AND SWIM TOWARDS THE ANODE, WHICH IS HELD BY THE OPERATOR. NEAR THE ANODE THEY ARE STUNNED AND CAN BE NETTED OUT OF THE WATER. THE FISH WILL QUICKLY RECOVER, AND CAN BE MEASURED BEFORE RETURNING THEM TO THE WATER.

July and, with twenty-four hours of daylight, must make the dangerous journey to the sea in full view of predators such as pike or terns.

The physiological and biochemical control of the parr-smolt transformation and the environmental factors affecting the migration to the sea, along with the behaviour of the fish, have been the subjects of a huge number of studies over the last twenty years, involving research teams throughout Europe and Canada. The result is that, despite the complexity of some of the changes that smolting entails, this is now probably the best understood part of the salmon's life.

SURVIVAL IN THE RIVER

When the smolt finally reaches the sea, it is likely to be one of only a handful of survivors from the original redd. For every smolt in the estuary, 50–100 eggs were probably laid in the gravel, the greater proportion of this mortality having occured in the first year of life. One study indicated that only between 5% and 30% of the hatched fry may survive the first feeding period, for failure to find a suitable territory or a shortage of food may account for many young salmon. However, these are not the only problems facing these fish.

There is no shortage of hungry stomachs which would welcome a parr. A keeper or bailiff would point an accusing finger at birds like the saw-bill ducks – the goosander and merganser – or alternatively the heron, and all have certainly ended up decorating a keeper's gibbet. While goosanders do undoubtedly take considerable numbers of parr and smolts, such birds possibly get more than their fair share of attention as predators, purely because they are easily seen. Underwater and out of sight, pike may be equally culpable. Indeed, predation by pike is thought to have been instrumental in the evolution of smolt migratory behaviour in Arctic rivers, according to Russian biologists.

Not only goosanders and herons have suffered from game control. Dippers have been shot for robbing salmon eggs as they chased their insect prey under the fast-flowing

streams and rivers. Yet people are always reluctant to place blame on the real
culprit responsible for most damage to
freshwater salmon populations, man
himself. Industrial effluent, forestry operations, acid rain, hydroelectric schemes,
and water abstraction – a short list of
man's more deleterious activities which
adversely affect young salmon in rivers.

A SMALL SAMPLE OF SCALES MAY BE SCRAPED FROM THE PARR'S FLANK.
UNDER THE MICROSCOPE, THE CONCENTRIC PATTERNS OF THE CALCAREOUS
SCALES FORM GROWTH RINGS WHICH CAN IDENTIFY THE AGE AND GROWTH
RATE OF THE FISH.

A C I D   R A I N

Acid rain, a result of atmospheric
pollution from power stations, motor
cars and their like, has now been over-
shadowed by climatic warming in the news headlines, yet its harmful effects have left
most of southern Norway's rivers and lakes fishless. Britain, a major source of airborne
pollution, has also suffered: south-west Scotland and Wales both have fishless lochs and
lakes as a result of acidification. Acid rain influences rivers that run over igneous rocks
or naturally-acid soils, common in many of Britain's upland
areas – often those parts of the country where salmon naturally
occur. The acidified water appears to kill fish through its effect
on the chemistry of aluminium, a common element in soils. In
acid waters, aluminium is toxic to fish and prevents them from
maintaining the salt balance in their body fluids. The eggs and
alevins are most susceptible, but sudden flushes of acid water,
often associated with snow melt, have been the probable cause
of adult fish kills too. Not only are the fish themselves killed
by acid waters, but the food of parr, such as mayflies and
shrimps, will also die.

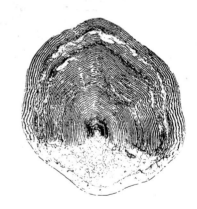

W A T E R   A B S T R A C T I O N

Water abstraction from rivers is also a major problem
and, as with acid rain, people are only just beginning to
appreciate fully the damage it can cause to fish populations.
Reductions in flow not only prevent the migration of adult fish
into or up a river but can also cause a massive loss of suitable
parr habitat, which may not be obvious to a casual observer.

A SALMON SCALE, COMPOSED OF
CALCAREOUS PLATES, SHOWS THE AGE AND
PREVIOUS SPAWNING HISTORY OF ITS OWNER.
THE WINTER CHECK ON GROWTH CAUSES
THE CONCENTRIC RINGS, OR ANNULI, TO BE
LAID DOWN CLOSER TOGETHER THAN UNDER
SUMMER CONDITIONS, ALLOWING AN
ESTIMATION OF AGE. THIS 14LB FISH HAS
SPENT 2 YEARS IN FRESHWATER, 3 YEARS AT
SEA AND SPAWNED TWICE.

Parr that are forced to flee their fast, shallow-water territories for the slower deep pools left during drought may well become more vulnerable to predation. Water abstraction affects different rivers in different ways, through variations in the levels of the water table and differences in gradient and configuration of stream beds. This means that it is very difficult to arrive at a standard minimum water-flow requirement for salmonids that could be applied to all rivers. Meanwhile, throughout the country the demand for water is increasing.

POWER GENERATION

Hydroelectric schemes have had a huge influence on European salmon stocks, particularly in Sweden and Finland. In Britain, hydro power was a contentious issue during the 1950s and 60s, though the effects have been relatively localised. The bare bed of the Perthshire River Garry in Scotland is ample testimony to the negative effects of water abstraction for power purposes. Dams and weirs, built to power the mills of the Industrial Revolution, were responsible for the destruction of much of Europe's salmon waters by blocking access to the spawning beds. The greedy belly of the goosander cetainly pales into insignificance compared with such human interference.

FORESTRY

In the 1980s, forestry became the contentious landuse issue in Britain, and one that has affected salmon populations. Commercial planting of conifers over large upland areas of Scotland and Wales has had a major effect on the drainage and water-flow characteristics of many river systems. Timber extraction operations can lead to the silting of spawning beds; destruction of redds can result from the flash flooding that occurs after drainage ditches are dug for tree planting; and dense plantations of trees, such as the much-maligned Sitka spruce, tend to accentuate the acidification of already acid soils and ground water. Foresters have fought strenuously to deny that their trees cause acidification, but it is now generally agreed that the trees will remove and concentrate the airborne nitrogen and sulphur oxides that eminate from industrial smokestacks and are the chemical cause of acid rain. However, by leaving the banks of streams clear from commercial planting, some of the acidifying tendencies of coniferous plantings can be minimised.

SMOLT SURVIVAL RATES

Assuming that the parr and smolt do survive all these hazards, how many such fish does a river produce and how might variations in this figure affect the number of

MAN'S COMMERCIAL ACTIVITIES HAVE HAD A HUGE UNINTENTIONAL IMPACT ON SALMON POPULATIONS, OFTEN
THROUGH INEFFECTIVE PLANNING PROCEDURES. WATER ABSTRACTION DOES NOT HAVE TO BE AS SEVERE AS THIS
EXAMPLE (RIVER GARRY, PERTHSHIRE) TO SERIOUSLY AFFECT SALMON POPULATIONS, AND U.K. FARMERS REQUIRE
NO PLANNING CONSENT TO REMOVE WATER FROM STREAMS. EVEN MORE EXTRAORDINARY IN THE U.K. IS THAT THE
HYDROLOGY OF WHOLE RIVER SYSTEMS, LET ALONE FISHERIES, HAVE ONLY RECENTLY FIGURED IN THE
LIMITED PLANNING CONTROLS THAT EXIST FOR COMMERCIAL FORESTRY, THOUGH SUCH LAND-USE HAS HAD
HUGE EFFECTS ON RIVER FLOW PATTERNS.

37

adults returning? The answer is that at least a threefold variation in smolt production can occur from year to year and, within certain undefined limits, high or low numbers of smolts leaving a river does not necessarily mean a correspondingly high or low number of returning adults. On a medium-sized river like the North Esk in north-east Scotland, for instance, the estimated numbers of smolts leaving the river every year from 1964 to 1984 varied between 93,000 and 275,000 per year, with possibly 16% to 40% surviving to return to coastal waters as adults. These estimated rates of production and sea-survival may be on the high side compared with other waters, and survival figures of between 5% and 20% are commonly quoted. More accurate data comes from fish-farmers who ranch salmon by releasing hatchery-reared smolts and harvest the returning adults. Such operations have at best only achieved return rates of 12%, though the fitness of hatchery-reared fish is likely to be less than their wild counterparts and so survival rates at sea might be lower for these domesticated salmon. Recently, the return rates of ranched Icelandic grilse have dropped from their norm of about 7% to only 1%, the level usually recorded for the two-seawinter fish. This known increase in mortality at sea coincides with low numbers of adult wild fish caught in recent years and indicates that all is not well with the salmon in the sea.

SEA-BOUND

Mortality at sea is variable enough to mask any clear relation between the number of migrating smolts and returning adults. A surprisingly high number do find their way back from the sea, and by the time the smolt next sees its home river it will be a very well-travelled animal indeed. Furthermore, it is a creature in which people will start to take a very close and, from the fish's point of view, somewhat unhealthy interest. But between leaving the river as a smolt and returning as an adult fish, the migrating salmon has a new environment to adjust to, and new dangers and opportunities to be faced – in short, a new life in the North Atlantic.

Life at Sea

If life was dangerous for the smolt in its downstream wanderings, it certainly becomes no easier on moving into the sea. There are a dozen hungry mouths which would make little distinction between, say, a herring, a mackerel, and a salmon smolt. Almost as though it senses this, the smolt is initially in no great hurry to escape the river's estuary. Drifting in and out with the tides, the fish may take a couple of days or more to acquire a taste for salt water and to shake off the world of river banks, channels, and the influence of fresh water.

A CHANGE OF WATER

While in the estuary, the smolt is still in easy reach of fishery scientists keen to find out what use of this environment the fish may make. A large number of these migrant fish have been tagged with little coloured plastic identity badges, the equivalent of the bird ring, in an attempt to identify the source of the fish if captured again. Other research groups have tracked smolts by fitting the fish with lightweight sonic tags, strapped panier-like to the fish's back. Carried by the tides, the tagged fish soon finds itself in its new salt-water home, followed by a team of tired workers listening to the tag's signals on hydrophones through day and night. The speed at which the smolt finds itself in sea water depends greatly on the chance of birth. In short-spate rivers, like those found on the west coasts of Scotland and Ireland, the fish may not have much of a chance to test the salt waters gradually, as there is such a short gradient between the freshwater outfall and the sea. By contrast, smolts born into larger river systems with their lengthy estuaries will have a much longer route to travel to the sea, and hence a slower transfer into full-strength sea water. Regardless of size of the estuary, once the smolt has the taste for salt water, it quickly heads out to sea and is soon lost to the fishery scientists.

However sudden the plunge, there is little doubt about the smolt's ability to cope with its change of environment. In fresh water the salt content of the water is very low in comparison with that of the fish's own body fluids; this condition is suddenly reversed when the smolt meets the salt water of the estuary. In fresh water the fish had to avoid losing its salts (mainly sodium and chloride ions) down the concentration gradient which

A Russian smolt, tagged and recovered from a power station in the Kola peninsula. The scales are easily lost and the underlying parr marks can be seen. Once in the sea, these fish are lost to biologists. What do they eat, what are the different causes of mortality and why is salmon survival at sea apparently so variable?

existed between the fish and the surrounding water. When this gradient is reversed, drastic action is necessary on the fish's part in order to stem the inexorable influx of salts into its body that will occur in sea water. The movement by osmosis of water between the fish and its surroundings is equally important. In the river the fish had had to cope with an influx of water into its body which was solved by producing copious quantities of urine. In the sea the smolt must now try to conserve its body water so as not to dehydrate in its new saline environment.

Paradoxically, the smolt actually starts to drink lots of this salt water, absorbing the salt from the water as it passes through the gullet and stomach. This excess salt is excreted back out of the fish through special cells in the gills, and the desalinated water left in the gut is absorbed into the body. This effectively provides the smolt with a replacement source of fresh water, all derived from a medium which, if it is full-strength sea water, is three times more concentrated in its salt content than the fish's own body fluids. The smolt is well prepared for this salt challenge by the time it reaches the sea. The salt-secreting cells in the gills, with their associated biochemical pathways, are all ready for operation before the smolt reaches the sea water of the estuary. In addition, deposits of organic-nitrogenous base compounds – guanine and hypoxanthine – have been laid down in the skin and the scales. These give the smolt its new silvery colours, typical of many marine surface-water fish, which suit the fish for a life on the ocean wave.

Some scientists consider the ancestral form of the salmon to have been a marine fish, and view this metamorphosis from parr to smolt as simply the fish's reverting to its ancestral physiological state.

To Eat or Be Eaten

The changes in the fish all mean that it is able to carry out its sea water task – to fill its belly and exploit the the rich feeding that was denied it in its previous rather austere habitat in the rivers. As any fish-farmer will tell you, the smolt wastes little time before feasting on whatever presents itself as food. Estuaries and coastal waters are very rich evironments where huge numbers of invertebrate animals such as shellfish, marine worms, and shrimps provide prey for a grand variety of birds and beasts. The smolt is unlikely to miss this chance and undoubtedly makes a good meal out of the mysid shrimps that abound and from other such animals.

Amidst this biological diversity there are plenty of new neighbours, not all of whom are friendly. The cormorant, a river estuary regular, which can force an outsize flounder down its gullet in the middle of winter, is unlikely to ignore a smolt in May or June. The handsome goosander with its long serrated bill, and the graceful tern which dips and darts over many estuaries, are both regarded as the smolt's 'enemies'. Any such predation is quite within the natural order, however, and there is little evidence to indicate whether such birds pose a serious threat to the salmon population. Substantial numbers of newly-tagged young migrant fish are reclaimed, not from some distant waterway but from nearby gull colonies. No doubt a smolt sporting a smart bright yellow tag is rather easier to see than one without, but it is hard to say exactly what effect such tagging may have. Certainly, some tagging teams have modified their tag colour schemes from yellow to a quieter green in an attempt to avoid unwanted attention!

Another major source of predation on smolts newly arrived in the sea are other fish species such as cole fish, pollack, and cod, whose young in turn may well be providing the smolt with a meal. Undoubtedly, the smolt will eat whatever shows itself and is probably quite wide in its tastes: young sand eels are a rich source of feed for many animals, from the less than graceful cole fish to the elegant tern. These food chains are complex and, being poorly understood, beg to have more research work done on them. The collapse of the sand eel populations in certain north Scottish waters in the late 1980s is an enigma to scientists. That this

THE GREY SEAL IS LARGER THAN THE COMMON SEAL, WHICH WAS THE MAIN CASUALTY IN THE RECENT MASS SEAL DEATHS IN THE NORTH SEA. GREY SEAL NUMBERS HAVE BEEN INCREASING – THE POPULATION IN 1989 IN BRITAIN WAS ESTIMATED TO BE A FIGURE OF 86,000 – BUT WHAT EFFECT DO THEY HAVE ON RETURNING SALMON? A COMMON SEAL NEEDS TO EAT ABOUT 8LBS OF FISH PER DAY, AND A GREY SEAL ABOUT 11LBS; BOTH SPECIES CATCH SALMON, THOUGH ON A RATHER LOCAL AND SEASONAL BASIS. THE SEAL CULLS OF THE 60S AND 70S – WHEN THIS PICTURE WAS TAKEN – WERE UNDERTAKEN TO PROTECT FISH STOCKS. PUBLIC PRESSURE STOPPED THE CULL – THERE ARE MORE VOTES IN SEALS THAN IN FISH.

SANDEELS FORM AN IMPORTANT PART OF THE MARINE FOOD CHAINS OF THE NORTH ATLANTIC, THE NORTH SEA AND THE BALTIC. NATURAL VARIATIONS IN ABUNDANCE OF SUCH FISH AND THEIR PLANKTONIC PREY CORRELATE WELL WITH CHANGING WEATHER PATTERNS IN THE ATLANTIC, PARTICULARLY WITH THE FREQUENCY OF WESTERLY WINDS. DO SUCH VARIATIONS AFFECT THE SURVIVAL OF SALMON SMOLTS IN THEIR FIRST MONTHS AT SEA? WHAT EFFECT WILL INCREASING LEVELS OF MAN-MADE GREENHOUSE GASES HAVE ON SUCH WEATHER PATTERNS, AND HENCE ON THESE FOOD CHAINS?

has had a catastrophic effect on sea-bird populations in these areas is well appreciated, but what effects might there be on the growth and survival of young smolts in these waters? The only certainty is that no one really knows the answer. Nevertheless, people are already pinning the blame for the poor runs of salmon seen in the early 90s on a lack of sand-eels.

UNKNOWN HABITS

Further questions arise now as the young salmon moves through the northern European coastal waters in these first summer months of life at sea. What exactly is the young fish eating? How is the fish navigating its way to its subsequent feeding grounds? Indeed, what path does it actually follow? The difficulties of investigating this part of the life-cycle mean that relatively little is known about these and other such matters, and our knowledge about these wild 'post-smolts', as the young salmon in their first summer months at sea are known, is patchy to say the least. Such gaps in our knowledge undoubtedly maintain the air of mystery that surrounds the fish, but they are certainly frustrating for those concerned with its conservation.

Salmon at sea appear to feed on shrimps, squid, and various fish such as capelin or menhaden – the so-called 'industrial fish' species – which are also caught by middle-water and deep-sea fishing boats in order to provide fish meal for non-human consumption. The dismal record of our exploitation of fish stocks in all seas and at all times, which has led to the collapse of many fish populations around the world, means that worry about the indirect effects of industrial fishing on salmon feeding and survival at sea is probably quite justified. Recent salmon catches in certain British rivers have included thin, poorly-conditioned fish that have suffered a complete lack of growth in their last few months in the sea. This raises the possibility that the fish have simply starved on their feeding grounds. So it is important to know where the salmon feeds and on what in these unknown months at sea.

T H E   F A R O E S

We do know that the young salmon of European stock head north through the North Sea and the Atlantic for, by the late autumn months, they have formed the base for a high-seas fishery off the Faroe Islands. The Faroe Islands, lying halfway between the Shetlands and Iceland, are half forgotten or ignored by many people in Britain today. The steep cliffs and shattered sea-stacks are an impressive home for millions of sea birds and some 40,000 people who, with little flat ground for agriculture, have always worked the sea. The Irish monk, St Brendan, is thought to have landed here on his sixth-century transatlantic tour. How much he drifted and how much he sailed is hard to say, but the same currents that pushed his oxhide boat to the Faroese Isle of Mykines probably carry the young salmon from the British and Irish coasts today.

When the research vessel 'Jens Chn Svabo' set her long lines in 1968 she inaugurated the controversial Faroese high-seas fishery, which at its peak in 1981 involved forty-four Danish and Faroese boats landing over 1000 tonnes of salmon. The initial catches were of young salmon in their first year at sea, but having looked around for bigger and better prey, the fishery moved to the north of the islands. Here in the Norwegian sea, many older and there-fore bigger fish were found, probably of

THE ISLE OF MYKINES IS PROBABLY THE BIRD ISLE RECORDED BY ST BRENDAN AND IS THE CENTRE OF THE RICH FAROESE FISHING GROUNDS WHERE SO MANY EUROPEAN FISH ARE FOUND IN THEIR FIRST WINTER AT SEA.

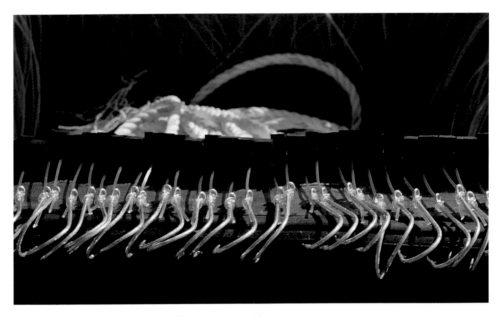

LONGLINE HOOKS AWAIT BAITING. WILL SUCH HOOKS CONTINUE TO BE USED FOR SALMON OR WILL ANGLERS
CONTINUE TO RAISE ENOUGH MONEY TO BUY OFF THE FAROESE FISHERMEN?

Scandinavian origin. These were consequently a much greater prize than the younger fish found further south, such stocks originating from British and Irish rivers. The fishery turned its efforts to covering the bulk of the Norwegian sea, but was restricted in the early 80s to that part of the Atlantic under the Faroese Government's control. This was a direct result of the establishment in 1984 of an international salmon management council, the North Atlantic Salmon Conservation Organisation.

The prize has to be good for these Faroese boats as, with a fishing season stretching from November to April, the North Atlantic is a hard place to work in. Setting their long lines with dozens of hooks baited with spratts, the boats find their best catches at dawn and dusk. Gutted and deep frozen, the fish make their return journey south or east in a manner they could not have anticipated. Conservationists and angling bodies in other parts of Europe are now trying to close down this fishery by paying the Faroese fishermen compensation for earnings lost through not fishing. Always a controversial subject, the Faroese fishery now intercepts fewer Scottish and Irish salmon than it did in the 1970s, and the catch quota of approximately 600 tonnes per year is mainly composed of Scandinavian fish. In recent years boats have landed only about half the allowable quota; this is largely due to a decline in fishing effort. The worldwide slump in salmon prices, a direct result of the massive over-production from salmon farms, has led to poor financial returns for the boat owners. It has been easier in the 1991/92 season for these fishermen to take the anglers' million pound three-year compensation package than to carry on long-lining for salmon.

THE GREENLAND BANKS

By the time the fog banks roll in as the cold Arctic air meets the warmer Atlantic waters, the salmon are apparently moving away from these Faroese feeding grounds. From June onwards, those fish aiming for an early return to their home rivers around the north and west European coasts are eagerly awaited by netsman and angler alike, while those that are destined to spend two or more winters at sea are starting to appear in a high-seas fishery off the west Greenland coast. This fishery has a longer history than the Faroese one, having operated since the late 50s. Initially it was a purely coastal net fishery, but by the mid 60s monofilament nets were being used up to forty miles offshore over much of the Greenland coast. A peak of 2689 tonnes in 1971 had crashed by the early 1980s to a tenth of this, well below the allowable catch agreed by international convention. The fish simply disappeared in 1983 and again the questions remain unanswered: have climatic and oceanic changes altered the fish's migration pattern? Are fewer fish spending two or more winters at sea, leading to fewer fish in Greenland waters?

TIME TO RETURN

The fish that appear off the west Greenland coast tend to be female, called 'multi-seawinter' fish by those in the salmon business. Though they are found entering our rivers in all seasons, it is really only these fish that make up the salmon catches in the first half of the year. Their smaller brethren that elect for just one winter at sea will only return to the rivers in the summer and early autumn. They are known as 'grilse', a category that most of the males fall into. This gives rise to yet more questions. How, when, and why do they 'decide' to adopt one or the other strategy? How do they navigate in the right direction according to their choice, say, of Ireland or Greenland?

We can guess at some of the answers. That multi-seawinter fish are mainly female, and that males tend to mature after only one winter at sea, is presumably due to the benefits that an early or late spawner enjoys relative to reproductive potential, growth, and the risks of mortality. The larger the female, the more eggs she can produce and the more offspring she might leave behind. Therefore she is likely to go for a long growing period in the sea so as to increase her body size and reproductive potential, despite the uncertain risks of mortality involved in staying on in the ocean.

There are few benefits to be obtained by a male in this manner, as sperm production is not really limited by body size. He is more likely to adopt an early spawning strategy at the expense of growth. In addition to this obvious trade-off, the growth rate at sea determines the timing of the return to the rivers in a manner that is not clearly understood. Fast-growing fish do tend to mature early – but not invariably; a genetical influence also exerts itself to some degree. Moreover, as if the picture were not complicated enough already, there is evidence that the growth rate of the parr in fresh water and its age of smolting are possibly connected with the timing of return.

This whole area of investigation is of the greatest interest to the angler, who is keen to see as many large, multi-seawinter fish return to the rivers in the early part of the year as possible; the smaller grilse returning in the summer months are less favoured. The proportion of fish that adopt one or other strategy has varied over the decades, and the subject has attracted much speculation about its controlling factors. Evidence exists for a northerly limit to the fish's distribution in the Atlantic, effectively set by a minimum sea temperature of 4°C. The temperature of the sea and, in particular, the position of this 4°C 'barrier', may then influence the feeding grounds open to the fish and hence their growth and maturation rates. If this is so, then the proportion of fish returning as large or small fish may well depend on climatic change. Large multi-seawinter fish, according to one theory, are thought to have been more numerous during warmer periods in the past. Thus, sunspot activity or carbon dioxide emissions could be justly credited by fishermen thankful for a successful day's fishing early in the season.

NAVIGATION AT SEA

Whichever decision the fish has made, it still must navigate itself correctly, either to further feeding grounds or else back to the home river. Here again, confusion reigns

AN INFAMOUS DANISH LONGLINER OF THE NORTH ATLANTIC – THE ONCLE SAM – AVOIDED INTERNATIONAL QUOTAS BY REFLAGGING TO PANAMA WHEN DANISH BOATS WERE BANNED FROM THE GREENLAND AND FAROESE SALMON FISHERIES.

over how the salmon manages. How is it possible to navigate across a seemingly vast and unchanging seascape without getting lost? St Brendan managed it, using currents, winds, and probably stars. Perhaps the Atlantic is not so featureless after all. Maybe the salmon can detect the ocean's currents through its electromagnetic fields and the potentials generated across such currents. Scientists have recently identified minute particles of magnetite in the fish's head, which could act as a miniature compass. Perhaps it uses the sun as a clue. Whatever form it may take, there might be a 'map' that the fish could follow by instinct, and the grilse or salmon, by adopting one or other attitude to its own map-reading of the Atlantic, may find itself unwittingly either back near its home coast or else approaching the Greenland banks.

The unerring accuracy of so many animal migrations is a marvel to most folk, but salmon do very occasionally go awry in their travels. Fish in their second summer at sea from French, British, or some other European waters, will find themselves sharing feeding grounds with their North American counterparts. Tagging has shown that fish do occasionally cross the Atlantic for good, running up a Newfoundland river rather than the rivers of their birth in Europe.

However, the salmon on its home run normally shows an uncanny knack of finding the river of its birth, though it may go through quite a period of trial and error before reaching home waters. If the fish has been following ocean and tidal currents, these may bring it to land hundreds of miles short of its ultimate destination. According to tagging results, over 90% of the fish caught in the Northumberland coastal fishery are destined for Scottish rivers, from the Tweed to the Aberdeenshire waters. Similarly, fish intercepted off the Donegal coast in Irish waters are often headed for Scottish west coast rivers. Yet again, fish tagged off the north-west of Scotland have reappeared on the east side of the country.

MEMORISING SMELLS

The fish's ability to find its home river out of the dozens it may pass seems utterly remarkable, but the vast majority of fish do select the river of their birth for their spawning run. Here the fish uses its memory, for as it left the river as a smolt it 'imprinted' to characteristic chemicals in its home stream. A year or more later, the fish actually 'remembers', or responds to, river water that it last tasted all those months before. There is ample evidence to show that this is the case, but no-one knows for sure what type of chemical odour the fish uses for its imprinting. Some say that it is odours from other fish in the river, characteristic to each stock, while others think that it could be aspects of the soils or rocks that taint the water. The salmon has a nose quite as sensitive to odours as a dog, fox, or deer, and smells will taint the water just as they will carry on the air. This makes it all the more remarkable that salmon can stomach swimming up rivers like the French Loire or the English Ribble, which are more akin to sewers than to the clean waterways they should be.

Though the type of chemical used by the fish in the identification of the home river is unknown, the method by which the chemical operates on the fish's behaviour seems reasonably straightforward and has been well studied in the related Pacific species. Salmon show a tendency to face into and swim against a water current, regardless of

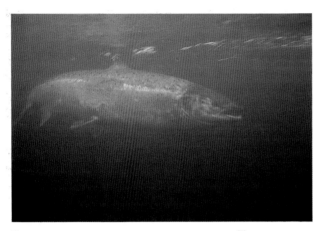

RETURNING SALMON ARE ATTRACTED TO FRESH WATER. THE FISH MAY LIE
IN THE FRESH WATER FLOW THAT OVERLIES THE DENSER SEA WATER IN
THE ESTUARY, WAITING FOR AN INCREASE IN FLOW TO
DRAW IT UP INTO THE RIVER.

whether it is salt or fresh water. This behaviour is enhanced by the presence of the 'home stream' chemical. If a fish accidentally swims past its home tributary, the absence of the imprinting odour in the water will diminish the fish's inclination to swim against the current and the fish will then drop back downstream until it meets the home waters again.

Having access to the commercial coastal nets in Britain, scientists have taken advantage of the relative availability of the fish to try to answer some of the hows and whys of the salmon's coastal wanderings. Some Scottish scientists have used ultrasonic tags that measure the compass direction of the fish's movements, while others have looked at the oxygen levels and salinity of the water surrounding the tagged but free-swimming fish. Studies such as these have shown, for instance, how fish will move into and out of river discharges for only a matter of seconds for what is presumably a 'tasting' exercise as they seek their home river. Such work has also demonstrated the behaviour of fish in different estuaries as they wait for a spate to draw them upstream, and their tolerance to deoxygenated waters, often a result of sewage pollution. The former Water Authorities in south-west England and southern Wales have funded numerous tracking studies of salmon swimming through the regions' polluted estuary waters.

NETTING

The tracking work has also shown the relative inefficiency of the various coastal nets, a feature actually maintained by law in both Norway and Britain to allow adequate escapement of spawning fish. Tagged fish will avoid salmon cobles and apparently swim across and around the fixed stake nets which still stretch across some beaches on the east coast of Scotland. These nets, and the bag nets off shore, are a fast-vanishing sight in the United Kingdom as this netting industry declines. The many old bothies and the drying greens for the nets around the coast bear silent testimony to this contraction. Both nets operate in a similar manner, with the fish encountering a leader net hanging from the surface of the water, the line of which it follows, passing eventually into a net trap from which it can be removed by the fisherman. These old-fashioned static nets allow the fish to see and often avoid them, in comparison with the invisible monofilament nets hung like curtains offshore, both by licensed boats in the Northumberland and Irish coastal fisheries and by an unknown number of illegal operators. These nets are frighteningly efficient as the fish cannot see them, particularly if fished at night, and the few fish that do meet and escape the nets show deep gashes where the nylon has cut into the flesh. So extensive is this illegal netting that a majority of fish in some Irish and Scottish waters show such net marks.

SALMON IN THE SEA MIGRATE CLOSE TO THE SURFACE, AND THIS HELPS THE FISHERMAN TRAP THEM IN HIS NETS. BY CONTRAST, SALMON FEEDING IN THE HIGH SEAS MAY BE FOUND DOWN AS FAR AS 100 METRES DEEP AS THEY SEARCH FOR THEIR PREY.

Once into the estuary, the fish is still sought after by netsmen operating sweep, drift, or seine nets, set from a small boat or coble and gathered into the shore. Like the off shore nets, these nets are not fished at the weekend or through a close season from late August or early September through to February. Rules also govern their operation to ensure their relative inefficiency to allow some escapement of spawning stock.

Netting has long been part of European estuary and coastal life, and it must be sad to see the traditions die as prices and catches have declined and political pressure has mounted on this old industry. However, many angling interests have looked with dismay from their riverside vantage point at what they have perceived to be the removal of large numbers of fish, trapped in and off estuaries during drought conditions. Any decline of the netting industry causes few tears to be shed in these ranks.

A   R U N N I N G   F I S H

Having found its home river, the salmon must await a reasonable flow of fresh water to draw it finally out of the sea. The fish responds clearly to changes in river flow and may lie offshore until a spate brings a deluge of coloured fresh water to its nose. In bigger estuaries, the fish may drift in loose shoals in and out with the tides, waiting for an increase in river flow to set the migratory urge off again. But when the spate does come, the fish wastes no time and is soon well past the tidal reaches of the estuary.

Thus the fish makes the transition once again into fresh water. Like the smolt, the salmon or grilse is truly able to live in both fresh or sea-water, and a sudden jump from one to the other is no problem. A jump it may quite literally be, as anyone knows who

49

has watched grilse clearing the river falls tumbling straight into the sea at Abhainnsuidhe on the Isle of Harris off the west coast of Scotland.

Whatever the mode of entry into a river, the fish is now described as 'fresh-run'. 'Running' is very much part of the peculiar language concerned with the salmon. Thus 'late-run' fish are those that have chosen autumn as the time of river entry; alternatively, there are also 'spring-run' and 'sea-run' salmon, and so on.

T H E   K I N G   O F   F I S H

The grilse, which entered the sea fourteen months earlier as a one-ounce smolt, now weighs a solid six or seven pounds as it chooses its river in the height of summer, while its multi-seawinter brethren might be up to five or six times this weight. But whatever its size, the silver-flanked fish is well worthy of the accolade 'the King of Fish'. Being royalty ensures an eager audience, and whether it be as a meal for a seal or a catch for the netsman or angler, the return of the salmon and grilse to our coastline is always welcome.

THE OLD WINCH AND DRYING GREEN POLES ARE ALL THAT IS LEFT OF AN OLD NETTING STATION, CLOSED THROUGH LACK OF FISH AND FALLING PRICES (RIGG, ISLE OF SKYE, SCOTLAND).

Back to the River:
The Lure of Angling

There can be few better sights than a fresh-run salmon splashing up through the shallows and gliding into the calm waters of the lowest pool in a river. As the bow wave slowly disappears, the fish is leaving the estuary and life at sea behind. The salmon is at last 'back home'. Now in the river it becomes the subject of folklore and anecdotes, equally mixed with fact and supposition. The willingness of anglers to tolerate the Scottish midge or the Norwegian mosquito on a July evening or to stand up to their waists in freezing waters in February – sure signs of insanity were it not for the lure of the fish – bear witness to this never-ending fascination with the salmon.

BIOLOGICAL CHANGES

The fish coming into the river has ultimately one aim and that is to spawn, and its behaviour and body chemistry are geared to this end. To our eye, the most obvious result of the process of maturation is yet another change in the colour and shape of the fish. The spring-run salmon or summer grilse enters the river coloured rather as it left as a smolt, with a blue-black back and silver-white sides – a fresh-run fish. After a few weeks in fresh water the fish loses its shining colours and becomes a greyer beast, being dismissively described as 'stale'. By September the fish will be showing its spawning colours, the reds, purples, browns, and blacks of autumn, more akin to a brown trout, and earning the fish its title of 'tartan fish' or 'kipper'. Together with this colour change the male or 'cock' fish develops the characteristic hooked jaw, the 'kype', a tool for close-quarter fighting for the right to mate on the spawning beds.

By the summer, the reproductive organs, or 'gonads', are developing quickly and filling out the body cavity of the fish. This and the external changes of shape and colour are controlled by the hormones of the pituitary and thyroid glands and by those of the gonads themselves. Such glands have an annual rhythm of activity, the timing of which is set by the day length of the season. The hormones stimulate the growth of the gonads, which in turn produce the sex steroid hormones. The function of these steroids is to govern the change in colour of the skin and the development of the male kype.

A FRESH RUN GRILSE ENTERS A RIVER POOL.

The effect of these biological changes is to get the fish onto the spawning grounds of the rivers and streams during November and December and into January. The changes brought on by maturation lead the fish back into a true freshwater existence. As maturation progresses, the fish will lose, at least in part, its ability to cope with the salt and water balance requirements needed for life in sea water. The resulting 'uneasiness' in sea water is probably a good mechanism for ensuring that the fish moves into the river to spawn. There is some evidence that, as the fish becomes more mature and approaches the time for spawning, it actually takes less stimulation from freshwater flow to coax the fish out of the sea and up into the river. Though the fish will mature if kept in salt water, it would rather seek a freshwater habitat – in anthropomorphic terms, it may feel more comfortable there.

THE TIMING OF RETURN

Despite the time schedule of maturation, salmon arrive back at our coasts and enter the rivers at all times of the year. True, the largest return occurs with the coming of the grilse in summer months, but a variable number of fish come into fresh water in all months, depending on the size of the river. Since the 1980s an increasing number of fish have been entering British rivers in the autumn and winter months, with a reduction in the spring and early summer seasons. Thus we can find fish arriving in our rivers at all stages of maturity. It is a subject that has long fascinated the fisherman naturalist.

Given that the fish does not eat in fresh water, what on earth makes a salmon enter a river possibly a whole year before it will spawn? Why the self-imposed starvation? It seems almost inconceivable to us with our pangs of hunger if tea is an hour late, that this fish will not eat for ten or eleven months, and after that still be interested in reproduction! But that is what happens, for the fish in fresh water ceases feeding and its gut atrophies and eventually shrinks. Occasionally the remnants of food are found in stomachs of salmon in rivers, and freshwater parasites have been found in the gut, presumably taken in with food. But, to all intents and purposes, the adult salmon in fresh water goes in for a long, long fast.

This lack of appetite in fresh water engenders discussion and disbelief. Why does a fish take a lure if it is not feeding and how can an animal last so long without food? Certainly, when grilse first arrive back in June or early July on the Scottish, Irish, and Norwegian coasts they are feeding on sand eel and similar fare. But by late July fish caught at sea contain no remnants of food in their stomachs, and this fasting continues in the river. The loss of appetite is associated with the advanced stages of maturation in all salmonids, and in the case of the salmon the fish on its spawning run is entering a habitat where the only available feed may be the young parr and smolts of younger generations.

Why not simply stay in the sea, carry on feeding, and enter the river nearer the spawning season? Here the answer becomes speculative, but we must assume that a strategy of a long freshwater residence does not actually carry any dire penalties for the fish. In the case of the United Kingdom, these early-running fish are very much associated with the big rivers such as the Tay, the Avon, and the Spey, and, as tracking studies on the Spey have indicated, it seems probable that such fish move into a suitable deep pool. Here they may stay for several months in the semi-torpid state that salmon seem able to adopt in fresh water, appearing to be in a trance with possibly a very low metabolic rate. Being cold-blooded beasts, this rate will be lower in winter than in summer when

A COCK SALMON SHOWS ITS AUTUMN COLOURS AS IT STRIVES TO REACH THE SPAWNING GROUNDS.

No words can adequately describe the thrill of catching a salmon — or the despair of losing one. Here both emotions are seen, as two fish are hooked but only one is landed (River Tay, Scotland).

the higher temperatures speed up the metabolism and greater energy is required just to keep the animal alive. By calculating the energetic costs of these metabolic rates, it is possible to show that a fish entering the river in March could lose 15% of its original body weight by October compared with one coming into fresh water in July, whose loss is likely to be 11% of the original weight. But if the July-running fish cannot enter the river due to low water flow and has to wait for autumn floods, then there might be very little difference in the weight loss between it and the March-run fish when the extra costs of swimming are taken into account.

The salmon does need reasonable river flows to attract it into the river out of the estuary. With drought a very real possibility in the summer season in many European waters, fish may be prevented from entering the river for several months. The problems of parasites, seals, and the attentions of man make this a risky option. Perhaps the danger of drought provides, at least in part, the reason that fish will run into fresh water in the winter or spring, so long before they are due to spawn. High river flows are almost guaranteed in these seasons and the fish's early entrance to the river may be part of a natural selection strategy to ensure survival of the 'family' line.

The habit of early running and spending more than one winter at sea is under both genetic and environmental control. As is seen in farmed fish, late-maturing, multi-seawinter salmon are more likely to produce similar multi-seawinter offspring than are grilse parents, illustrating a clear genetical control. But there is also a probable environmental influence on this timing of return, through the effect of growth rate on maturation.

The exact balance between the genetic and environmental components of control has yet to be determined. For instance, it appears that it could be the high, cold head-waters of big rivers that produce the parr destined to become the valuable multi-seawinter fish. But is this simply because these tributaries are where such fish spawn, and so are we just seeing the genes' influence? Or is it that slow growth conditions produced by such an environment somehow encourage fish to spend more than one winter at sea? If so, what effect will climatic warming have on these fish through its raising of river temperatures? Whatever the answer, this perception by the fish of its performance in a habitat, with the resulting variations in its life-story, is of key scientific interest and preoccupies researchers on both sides of the Atlantic.

ANGLING

As to why a salmon in the river takes an artificial fly, worm, prawn, or spinner – this is something, thankfully, that does not lend itself to scientific investigation very easily. It is likely to remain the subject of numerous individual theories for many years to come! This question is bound up with the limitless lore and millions of words written on how and when to catch the fish. A momentary surge of blood to the head, an aggressive snap, or the blind reaction to distantly remembered food – whatever it may be, the state of mind of the salmon as it sucks in the worms is and will remain one of the fish's best-kept secrets.

Angling for fish of any type has long been one of Europe's most popular activities, and though salmon fishing is quite definitely at the luxury end of the sport, people from all walks of life can gain access to waters where salmon swim.

Fishing with an artificial fly is generally considered the most gentlemanly way of landing the fish, and its many devotees consider it more an art form than a sport. Certainly, casting a fly is a delightful pastime, and the excitement of playing a fish on the excellent, lightweight fly tackle available today is unbeatable. Casting down and across a holding pool, the fisherman aims to pull his fly across the nose of his quarry. Commonly, the fish will swirl at the fly but not take, and this may be repeated several times before contact is made.

The fisherman needs to fish his fly particularly close to the spring-run fish as it lies on the bottom, and a weighted line will sink the lure. These early-run fish, being on average large and rather scarce, are the most highly prized salmon to catch. The smaller grilse found in the rivers in summer are less valued by the serious fishermen, but the lively fight they put up to gain their freedom means they are an excellent quarry.

The artificial flies the fishermen use are themselves artful creations. With names like 'Blue Charm', 'Hairy Mary', and 'Thunder and Lightning', the gaudily-coloured flies are well designed to entice the salmon to 'take'. Many of the beautiful patterns are lost or

WITH THE RIGHT WATER CONDITIONS, JUMPING ACTIVITY AT FALLS CAN BE QUITE INTENSE. FISH START THEIR JUMP NEAR THE SURFACE WITH A SINGLE BEAT OF THEIR TAIL, USING THE UPCURRENT FROM THE STANDING WAVE BELOW THE FALLS TO GIVE THEM THE NECESSARY LIFT. JUMPING ONLY TAKES PLACE IN DAYLIGHT AS THE FISH AIMS FOR THE CONTRAST BETWEEN THE WATER AND THE SKY IN ORDER TO GAUGE THE HEIGHT OF THE JUMP ACCURATELY.

ignored now, and modern flies, one imitating a shrimp for instance, are now luring the fish to the angler's net.

Despite the appeal of fly fishing, many anglers take the fish by spinning an artificial lure through the water. Metal spoons and spinners, including the popular toby, and little wooden dummy fish with vanes attached, known as 'Devon minnows', are designed to turn in the water when reeled in past the fish and are favoured in large rivers or flood waters. But the humble earthworm or the prawn, stuck on a hook, still lures many fish to the bank. Fished in waters that are slightly coloured through a spate, the bunch of worms is slowly sucked in by the fish and the animal is often hooked deep in its gullet. Little wonder, then, why people find it hard to believe that the fish is not feeding.

Whatever the method, there always seems to be a large element of luck involved in catching a salmon. Trout fishermen like to think that their particular branch of the sport requires more skill, as the feeding trout must be fooled into taking the lure. Not so the salmon, they say. However, a good salmon fisherman will know what size of fly to fish in certain water conditions, where to put his fly, and how deep to fish it. But perhaps more than anything else, it is important to be in the right place at the right time, and this involves having reasonable access to the river or lake when the fish are there and the water conditions are right.

Fish that are just beginning or have just finished moving through a part of the river system seem more likely to snap at a fly, and so it is important to know which water conditions will make fish move. According to tracking studies, fish are most active at night, and dawn and dusk are often worthwhile times to get on to the water. Once they have started to run upstream, the fish are often blind to anything hurled at them, much to the angler's frustration as he sees countless fish moving past him and knows that upstream, where the fish finally halt, someone is making a killing.

T H E   S A L M O N   L E A P

When a fish does run, it may cover forty kilometres before stopping again. For an animal that has been to Greenland and back, swimming up the length of the Tay or the Tana presents no great difficulty. And it is when the fish are running upstream and they come to one of the waterfalls across their path that they meet with their widest and most admiring public.

Launching themselves up and into a seemingly impassable cascade of white water, the salmon never seem to give up, despite repeated failures to gain the upper waters. When a fish does get a purchase with its tail in the plume of falling water and manages to force itself up, the lucky spectator will feel like applauding the achievement.

The salmon use the upcurrents of the standing wave below a waterfall to give themselves the acceleration to jump their best efforts of ten or twelve feet. When they hit the water after a jump, their tail starts to beat at full speed. At top speed a large fish can swim at five or more metres per second and can keep this up for about ten to twenty seconds. So if only the fish can get its tail and body into unbroken water to give it purchase, it can make headway up very fast-flowing torrents. Sometimes a small sea trout will barge its way past a much bigger salmon which is trying desperately to clear the top of a fall, just because the trout's smaller size allows it to get that necessary grip on the water. A poor sense of direction when jumping can mean a hard landing on a bare

A POACHER'S MONOFILAMENT GILLNET BLOCKS A SCOTTISH WEST HIGHLAND RIVER. IT IS ILLEGAL TO FISH WITH SUCH A NET FOR SALMON AND, SINCE 1986, ILLEGAL TO CARRY ONE IN SCOTTISH COASTAL WATERS — YET IT IS NOT AN OFFENCE TO OWN ONE. SUCH NETS CAN BE BOUGHT OPENLY ACROSS THE COUNTER IN FISHING SHOPS.
RECENT LEGISLATION IN SCOTLAND HAS BEEN AIMED AT CLOSING THE POACHER'S SALES OUTLETS — PRINCIPALLY HOTELS — BY MAKING IT AN OFFENCE TO BE IN POSSESSION OF SALMON WHICH CANNOT BE REASONABLY PROVEN TO HAVE BEEN LEGALLY OBTAINED.

rockface before tumbling back into the river. Whatever the result of the jump, the thousands of spectators who have watched salmon trying to clear the many falls in Scotland, Ireland, and Norway, cannot help but marvel at the blind instinct forcing the fish to try and try again.

On some falls, and more recently on dams, the fish have been given a helping hand in the shape of fish passes. Pitlochry dam in Perthshire, with its pass and underwater observation chamber, is probably the best known in Britain today, but the effort that has gone in to helping fish past such obstacles is not just a recent phenomenon. From the mid-nineteenth century, fish passes were erected on many Norwegian and Scottish falls to allow fish access to the upper river. Just upstream from the Pitlochry dam, on the Falls of Tummel, is a good example of these early engineering efforts: a 140 m pass, dating from the turn of the century, is tunnelled through solid rock to let the fish pass the difficult falls.

Many falls in Norway, Iceland, and Scotland, however, are just too great a height for fish passes. At Glen Muick in north-east Scotland, for instance, fish may be netted out and manhandled to the top to give them access to more spawning beds. Others are even too high for this, and smolts would have a rough time of it coming down falls like the Gullfoss in Iceland or even more modest ones, such as the Kirkaig Falls in the north of Scotland. Underneath such natural barricades quite large numbers of fish will congregate, and it is here that the temptation to do a spot of illegal fishing may be too much for some folk to resist.

POACHING

Poaching – the word conjures up different ideas to different people. To the regular fly-fisherman, the mere mention of poaching may cause apoplexy; to others, it suggests all the fun of fishing for one of the best prizes with the added excitement of illegality; and for professional gangs it is just good business, regardless of the consequences.

The notion of one for the pot – and probably one for the neighbours, too – still lingers on, and in many parts of the Scottish Highlands, for instance, the fridges and freezers are seldom without a fish taken in this spirit in the summer months. How on earth can a landowner lay claim to a fish which he may never have seen before, and is swimming free in God's world? This is how the argument runs in many respectable households.

Yet sadly this attitude means that people will often take no action against gangs killing fish by methods that are detested, such as using a cyanide chemical designed to gas rabbits. This poaching activity kills not only the adult salmon, but also alevins and parr as well as aquatic insect life, and leaves a truly desolate river behind. Together with netting, this kind of poaching is a long call from the notion of the noble poacher, out with his gaffe, outwitting the keepers and bailiffs.

Though the tools of the trade might have changed from spears, ripping hooks and gaffes to poison and gillnets, the battle of wits between the two sides of the law still goes on. Any idea of grudging admiration between the two opposing sides is long gone, and the hostility has often led to open 'war' and violence. Sunk fishery-protection boats, slashed car tyres, shooting incidents, arson, and beatings are not unknown. Still part of the romance of the salmon, the reality of poaching today can be anything but romantic.

S P A W N I N G

To the salmon in the river, about whom all the fuss is made, it makes little difference whether there is an angler, netsman, or poacher after it. The fish has been harried halfway across the seas and back again, and has to wait until late October or November before being left in peace. By then the fish is black, bronzed, and red, the males have the large kype, and the flesh of both sexes has become softer as body tissues have been converted into gonads. Having a higher water content, the flesh has a lower value than earlier, and fish caught in this state are often used for smoking. Perhaps it is just as well that all these changes take place, as the fish on their spawning grounds can be even more vulnerable to unscrupulous people than earlier in the season.

By late October and early November the maturing fish are gathering in those parts of the rivers that will be suitable as spawning beds. The main requirements are a fast-flowing supply of water and a stone size that the fish can lift and disturb. A wide range of gravel and stone sizes are used by fish to make the redds in which the eggs are deposited. Salmon undoubtedly do show preferences for sites with a certain water depth

A COCK FISH FOLLOWS A HEN AS SHE APPROACHES SPAWNING TIME, THOUGH THERE IS NO FAITHFUL BOND PAIRING BETWEEN THE SEXES.

A FRESH RUN SPRING FISH (UPPER) AND A KELT, CAUGHT IN MARCH IN GALLOWAY. THE FEMALE KELT MAY HAVE ENTERED THE RIVER LOOKING LIKE THE SPRINGER, BUT WILL HAVE LOST A QUARTER OR MORE OF ITS BODY WEIGHT THROUGH THE PRODUCTION OF EGGS AND A LONG STARVATION PERIOD. MALES LOSE EVEN MORE BODY WEIGHT THAN THE FEMALES THROUGH THEIR STRENUOUS REPRODUCTIVE ACTIVITY, AND THIS MAY EXPLAIN THEIR MUCH HIGHER POST SPAWNING MORTALITY RATE.

and velocity, and the tails of pools and shallow runs often give the right conditions. Fish will spawn right through a river system, wherever conditions are suitable, from just above tidal limits to some of the highest streams and tributaries.

Some of the most important biological questions that affect stock management are asked at this stage. How much competition is there for space on the spawning beds? Do late-spawning fish cause problems by overcutting redds and damaging earlier spawning efforts? Do fish spread out evenly through a river system? Will autumn-run fish, summer salmon, grilse, and spring-run fish spawn together or do they spawn in different sites and at different times? Initial tracking studies indicate that the fish do separate out to some degree, with the early-running fish using the headwaters of the river for spawning. These questions all prompt various popularly-held theories which have a tendency to be considered as fact, but the only real fact is how little information exists on these topics.

Male fish will remain on or near the spawning beds for quite a period of time, competing with other rivals for females that might be ready to spawn. Such cock fish may rest in the pools between the spawning gravels, coming into the beds when a female shows signs of cutting a redd. With fins erect and the great mouth wide open, the dominant male will threaten other males that venture too close. If that is not enough, actual snapping and biting will be the last resort, leaving scars and gashes. Fighting males may even disrupt the female as she prepares to cut her redd. These aggressive males will travel a few kilometres up or down the river in search of females, and vary enormously in their success rate as seducers.

CUTTING THE REDD

Pairs of spawning fish may be seen within a few yards of each other, but though the spawning behaviour patterns and characteristics are generally known, only a few detailed observations in the wild have ever been made. The male will try to approach a female fish which has started to show signs of cutting a redd. There is no faithfulness in their pairing, and a female may be escorted by a number of different male hopefuls while she starts her preliminary excavations. After various false starts over a couple of days or so, the female will start digging her redd by lying on her flank and lifting her tail up and down, using the currents created to lift and displace the stones. When a hole has been cut, the fish will lay her eggs, the male quivering and releasing his milt alongside her. After laying perhaps several thousand eggs, the hen fish will then cover the redd by lifting stones upstream of the redd. She may then cut another redd and lay more eggs, from a few hours to a few days later, until virtually all her eggs are shed.

Although the current may be almost a metre per second above the redd in midwater, close to the gravel in the bottom of the redd the water is slacker and the eggs will sink in among the stones. The eggs are incredibly tough, and for the first twenty-four hours after fertilisation they can stand a good deal of movement, so settling in the redd and being covered by stones which might be six inches in size presents no difficulty. Once in the redd, the main dangers to the eggs come from floods washing away the stones and possibly the disturbance of redds by subsequent spawning fish.

COUNTING THE STOCKS

The accurate homing of the salmon to its native river, and possibly to its natal tributary, means that it is in the river that different stocks separate out and can therefore be individually managed. It is now that the endless arguments start as to whether the stocks are up or down, who is catching too many, and why the fishing 'is a shadow of its former self'. One problem is that the only data on the stocks of most countries come from catch statistics, which cover only part of the year – what enters the rivers of Britain from November to January, for example, is unknown. Another difficulty is that assessing catch data properly requires a measurement of the effort and time involved in trying to catch the fish, and information on this is normally lacking. Catch statistics are therefore far from perfect data. In large river systems, such as the Scottish Tay, matters are further complicated by the probable existence of a number of separate stocks within the one system, each with possibly different characteristics and fluctuations in numbers. Last but not least, illegal fishing is widespread throughout European waters and is obviously unquantifiable.

It has long been the aim of many fishery scientists to assess the size of salmon stocks on individual rivers. France, England, Ireland, Norway, and Scotland all have electronic fish counters in operation on some of their smaller rivers, such as on the River North Esk on the Scottish east coast. Since 1980, this has given year-round records of the number of salmon and grilse entering and leaving this particular river. It has shown, for instance, that in 1981 less than 20% of the total stock entered the river in September and October, while in 1984 40% of the annual stock entered in these same months, thus demonstrating a trend towards autumn runs in Scottish rivers. However, much of this type of data never reaches the public, and even the catch statistics for the different fisheries do not reach a wide audience. A quick look at these figures could well explode a few myths, and it is a shame that they are not more widely circulated.

Comparison of catch data shows how much variation between river systems and a country's national trend there can be. The Scottish east coast River Dee, for instance, has shown a steady decline in both salmon and grilse catches by nets and rods since the early 1950s. Over this time the neighbouring Spey has been relatively constant, whereas the Tay to the south showed a 100% increase in the late 60s and 70s, followed by a drop back to the levels of the early 50s. The overall Scottish trend has been an approximate 30% increase coinciding with the Tay's rise, followed by a drop in the mid 80s to just below the figure for 1952–5. . The returns for the early 90s are showing a further drop to what is possibly an all-time low, probably caused in part by a low survival of fish in the sea and in part by a reduction in fishing effort, the result of a drop in the number of netting stations actually operating around the coast. Other countries have shown similar trends.

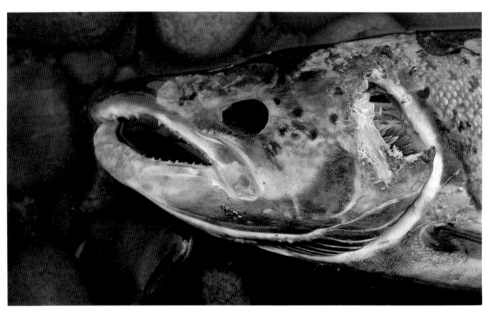

JANUARY – THE AUTUMN COLOURS OF THE KELT'S CARCASS SOON ROT AWAY AS A NEW GENERATION OF EGGS START THEIR DEVELOPMENT.

Salmon and Man: A European History

Salmon have long been appreciated in the countries of Europe. This appreciation, however, has had a background of confrontation, as one potential exploiter has competed with another for access to the salmon resource. The conservation movement has its roots in such disputes over resources, though initial protective measures for the salmon were taken for hard-headed commercial reasons rather than for any higher principle of conservation. But whatever the reason, this is not a new issue.

E A R L Y   R E C O R D S

The earliest records of any interaction between man and salmon date back some 25,000 years. The hunters of Stone Age Europe left reindeer antlers carved with the salmon's distinctive form outside their cave dwellings, while inside, the salmon was engraved on the walls alongside the bison and deer whose images are so familiar to us today. Indeed, the same style of picture of the fish and other game were still being drawn by Lapp hunters in northern Norway and Russia in the sixteenth and seventeenth centuries. There, the fortune teller of each village used a drum painted with animals to predict future hunting and fishing success.

Scotland is another country where salmon have long been valued, and not just for the food quality. The characteristic shape of the fish can be seen carved on Pictish symbol stones dating from the seventh century. The miraculous arrival of the fish in rivers from season to season, as well as its obvious sustenance value and aesthetic qualities, has ensured that the fish supports a strong symbolism, representing the fertility of the natural world. To the Celts, the salmon was the oldest animal in the world, and the source of wisdom itself.

Since medieval times the salmon has been prominent in European heraldry, a direct development of its use on the Pictish stones. Today in Scotland a symbol of the fish familiar to many people is found on the heraldic arms of the City of Glasgow – an ironic choice given the scarcity of salmon in the Clyde over the last hundred years or so, a direct result of pollution from the city itself.

THE OLDEST KNOWN REPRESENTATION OF A SALMON, IN THE CAVE KNOWN AS THE FISH SHELTER IN THE VEZERE VALLEY, PERIGORD.

LEGISLATION

Just as the importance of the salmon in prehistoric times is indicated by the appearance of the fish on symbol stones and in cave art, so, as soon as society became more ordered, the salmon quickly made its way on to the legal statute books. Both the Norse parliament of Viking society and, further south, the lawmakers of Charlemagne's rule passed edicts concerning the salmon. However, nowhere was legislative interest more evident than in Scotland, where the parliament in medieval times stands head and shoulders above other countries in terms of the number of laws made to conserve and regulate the salmon fishery.

Scottish legislation apparently started in the eleventh century. By the thirteenth century the export of dried, salted, and pickled salmon to England and the Continent was big business. Fixed traps and barricades across rivers, known as 'cruives', must certainly have been in place before the fourteenth century, when legislators, in a Scotland that had temporarily won peace from southerly neighbours, found time to pass rules governing such traps. In 1318 it was ordained that weirs and cruives must have an opening in the top of the barrier to allow smolts to pass through; failure to comply would land the owner in jail for forty days. Normally built of stone, a cruive was simply a barricade that would channel migrating fish into a trap of some sort. In 1424 King David of Scotland passed statutes ordering all cruives in estuaries to be completely pulled

A FEW ANCIENT FORMS OF NETTING STILL TAKE PLACE IN EUROPEAN WATERS — HERE A HAAF NETTER AWAITS A SALMON DROPPING DOWNSTREAM ON THE EBBING TIDE IN THE RIVER NITH, SCOTLAND. HIS NET IS MOUNTED ON A 16FT WOODEN FRAME WHICH HE MUST QUICKLY LIFT TO TRAP ANY FISH ENTERING THE NET. THE CENTURIES OLD HAAF OR HEAVE NETS ARE TERMED PUSH NETS, AND ARE NOW LIMITED TO THE SOLWAY RIVERS AND THE NEIGHBOURING RIVER LUNE. SIMILAR NETS - LAMP OR LAVE NETS - WERE FOUND UNTIL RECENTLY THROUGHOUT WALES AND SOUTH WEST ENGLAND.

down: 'all cruives and yairs set in wateris quhair the sea fillis and ebbis be put away and destroyed for ever mair'. In addition, fishery owners were reminded to keep the 'setterdais slop', or the Saturday close period. Legal definitions and language were clearly designed for every man to understand, hence a reference to gaps in cruives to be wide enough for a hypothetical pig to turn around in: 'the midst of the water should be fre sa mekill than ane swine of three zeir auld and well fed is of length and may turn him within it in sic manner that neither his grunzie nor his tail tuich any sides'. Lawyers had not yet got their hands on language! It was not until 1951 that cruives were completely banned in Scotland.

In England, salmon made an early appearance in law, through King John and the Magna Carta of 1215, which assured public right to the salmon fishery. English control of fishery methods was not as tight as Scottish, and it is entertaining to see that Scottish rules on the joint border waters were relaxed so as to give the Scottish fishermen the edge over their English rivals!

Spain also looked to legislation to protect and govern her salmon waters, apparently then as rich as any in Europe. Close seasons were introduced by King Alfonso el Sabio in 1258, and by the fifteenth century the rights to fish for salmon were keenly contested through the courts.

Further north, France, also a country with a considerable salmon resource, had a well-controlled salmon fishery right up to the Revolution of 1789. Before then much of the waters on her Atlantic coast produced rich pickings for the monasteries and the

EGGS AND MILT ARE SQUEEZED FROM WILD CAUGHT FISH AND MIXED IN A BOWL BEFORE TRANSFER TO THE HATCHERY, LATER TO BE RESTOCKED INTO THE RIVER. THE RELUCTANT PARENT FISH CAN THEN BE RETURNED TO THE WATER.

PICTISH
STONE,
DUNROBIN,
SUTHERLAND

aristocratic families, who rightly valued this prize fish. The disorder following the Revolution ensured free access for all to the salmon fishings but also, sadly, initiated the destruction of the fish populations through overfishing and the creation of weirs.

Behind all salmon legislation is, naturally, the thorny question of who has the right to take fish. The rights to fish for salmon in Scotland, for instance, have always lain with the Crown, and these rights, granted to different people on a permanent or temporary basis, are considered as heritable estates. So the owner of a river bank need not necessarily have the rights to the salmon fishings. Such written title allows the owner to fish for migratory salmonids, but does not give exclusive rights to the sedentary brown trout. By legal definition 'salmon' covers sea trout, but here the law can become confused, as sea trout is the same species as brown trout! If the law is being an ass, it can surely be excused in this instance, as confusion even over the connection between salmon and their parr was widespread until the mid-nineteenth century.

B U R N I N G   T H E   W A T E R

By 1696 Scottish legislators clearly saw a need to preserve stocks and limit the efficiency of fisheries, and in that year the parliament of Scotland strengthened the law conserving the salmon with legislation against 'Killers of Black Fish and Destroyers of the Fry and Smolts of Salmon'. One traditional method of catching the spawning or 'black' salmon – with the 'leister' or salmon spear – had already been outlawed, by 1533 in England and 1601 in Scotland. If there are problems nowadays with the enforcement of salmon laws and prevention of poaching, things were certainly no different following the banning of the use of the leister. For the next two centuries, the habit of 'burning the water' at night was widely recorded, with torches of tarred heather enabling the man handling the leister to see the salmon. No enforcement of the law was apparently undertaken, indeed a display of this sport was even laid on for Queen Victoria on the River Dee. The spearing of salmon was again outlawed in 1857, but even today it seems unlikely that the leister, or an updated version, has gone completely out of use.

R E S T O C K I N G

PICTISH
STONE,
GLAMIS,
PERTHSHIRE

It was in the nineteenth century that the present-day British organisation of salmon fisheries was fashioned. Rod and line fishing became a highly desirable sport: bag and stake net fishing began in coastal waters, and the Salmon Fisheries Acts of the mid-nineteenth century created the mechanism for fishery administration – the District Salmon Fishery Boards. These bodies, representing a range of owners' interests, have been responsible for managing and conserving salmon in each of their districts, and in Scotland it is still they who employ bailiffs and operate restocking programmes. In

This trade was revolutionised by the suggestion of a Scot, George Dempster, to use ice to pack the fish. Ice was subsequently collected in winter and stored in caverns underground in preparation for the summer catches. Later, the advent of rail and steamboats allowed easy access to the rapidly developing industrial markets. The islanders of Bornholm in the southern Baltic could have their salmon in the Paris market thirty-six hours after landing it, thanks to the steamer. Prior to this, spoilage of the fish must have been a common occurrence, and in Scotland one idea suggested by caring officials of the time was that such fish should be donated to the local lepers.

The nineteenth-century trend towards rod fishing on rivers led to a considerable change in how fish stocks were exploited in the remoter countries of the Continent. Up until this time, netting was the chief way to land large numbers of fish along the length of a river. In 1817 for instance, salmon were being caught commercially on rivers such as the Tummel in Scotland, and being sold for fourpence a pound in the towns. But this industry was soon to be limited to the estuaries as landowners were quick to realise the sporting value of such fisheries on the rivers themselves. Anglers from the south started to penetrate the Highlands of Scotland and the remoter parts of Ireland, and, in particular, discovered the great rivers of Norway. It did not take long for other nationalities to take up the general idea, and by the early twentieth century Americans, for instance, already owned large chunks of Norway's salmon rivers. The earliest practitioners of the sport at that time were British aristocrats and industrialists. Men such as the Duke of Roxburghe brought with them a good deal of money to these poorer parts of the world, and even in countries like France introduced the local populace to the art of fly fishing.

S P O R T I N G   R E C O R D S

Fishing using rod and line dates as far back as Egyptian times when Anthony, in an early fishing competition with Cleopatra, apparently had divers place live fish on his hooks, a tactic not available to most modern anglers! Anglers in the late eighteenth century started out after salmon using tackle that might be recognisable today. Anyone who has handled a Victorian greenheart sixteen-foot salmon rod realises that anglers of those days must have been supermen. Someone who could handle one of these heavyweight rods all day thoroughly deserved his or her catch – and what magnificent catches there were in the Victorian era. Over six days in 1888 a Mr Naylor and two companions on the Grimersta on Lewis took 333 salmon, weighing over 2000 lbs in total weight, and other such baskets are much recorded. Much of the lore of the fish originated in those times, with ghillies, drams, and tales of poaching.

It is interesting that in this male-dominated sport it was a woman, a Miss Ballantine on the River Tay near Caputh in 1922, who landed the largest rod-caught salmon in

FRESH FROM THE SEA, PANDEMONIUM REIGNS ON THE FLOOR OF THE COBLE BEFORE THE 'PRIEST' BRINGS PEACE. SHOULD THESE FISH HAVE BEEN LEFT FOR ANGLERS, AND HOW MANY OF THEM MIGHT HAVE BEEN CAUGHT BY ROD AND LINE?

Britain. This colossus, weighing in at 64 lbs, was outweighed by a fish of 70 lbs caught in the Tay nets at the turn of this century. Some claim the British record comes from the Thames – a monster of 83 lbs – but evidence of this record is lost. Perhaps the best 'record' comes from the Forth at the turn of this century – a giant of 103 lbs which, as it was poached, never received official recognition. However, the world record for a rod-caught salmon comes from the River Tana in northern Norway, where the local postman, Henrik Henriksen, caught a 79 lb fish in 1928.

Nowadays the sport is still very exclusive as far as some rivers go, but most folk can get a chance at a fish, if not the world record, on many of the smaller Scottish, Irish, and Norwegian rivers. The growing popularity of time-share ownerships extends not only to property but also to fishing rights, a development which has caused much anguish to many anglers. In Britain, however, a large amount of good salmon water is now owned or leased by angling associations, providing important access to salmon fishing for those who cannot afford the thousands of pounds-a-week rentals that the best beats command.

COASTAL NETTING

In addition to rod fishing, the other great salmon-fishing tradition over the last two centuries has been the coastal netting industry. Just as the river ghillie knows where his fish lies, the netsman knows how his nets will fish in certain winds and tides and in what riverflows the fish will be moving.

Stake nets on coastal beaches were developed in their present form in Scotland at the end of the eighteenth century, and by the start of the next century the right to place such nets in estuaries was already being challenged in the courts by netting interests upstream. The same style of net, but fished offshore – the bag net – appeared shortly afterwards in both British and Scandinavian coastal waters. These early bag nets were cumbersome affairs, cotton mesh coated with tar, supported with corks and tarred oak barrels as floats. A crew of at least four would have been required to handle these, but modern equipment means that netting stations today need only employ one or two men to man the nets.

With weekly and annual close seasons, these nets have been well regulated, but the fishing stations are now in decline. Catches waned during the 1980s and, perhaps more importantly, competition from farmed salmon forced prices down quite dramatically. Pressures on the industry have been increasing, and the weekend close period in British waters has just recently been extended, further reducing the ability of these stations to pay their way. Norway, too, has seen a dramatic contraction of her netting industry in her coastal waters, while 1989 finally saw the phasing out of the much criticised drift net fishery, and now only fishermen in the very north of the country, Finnmark, can fish any type of net in the sea for salmon.

R O D S   A G A I N S T   N E T S

In Britain, the Atlantic Salmon Conservation Trust, a charitable body formed in 1985, has been buying out the coastal netting stations and closing them down under the banner of 'conservation of the salmon', though they are in effect more concerned with increasing the share of fish available to the angler, rather than with its conservation. The motives and justification of such groups with charitable status have been questioned by those fighting a rearguard action on the netting industries' behalf. This reflects the antagonisms and tensions between the netting and angling bodies, both of whom in a perfect world should be able to work together with a common interest at heart, the conservation and rational exploitation of the Atlantic salmon.

Netting salmon in the sea is rightly described as an indiscriminate interceptory method of fishing, i.e. it affects fish from a number of different rivers and stocks. The same is strictly true for estuarine nets as well. Due to the discrete nature of salmon stocks from different rivers, the indiscriminate nature of these net fisheries is used by the angler as a reason to ban this type of fishing. The argument runs that it is only in the river that stocks separate out and hence can be individually managed. So far, so good. But in large river systems, angling as the main method of exploitation only crops about 10% of the available fish, allowing a spawning escapement that is probably well in excess of the percentage needed to maintain the population. The level of exploitation through angling may rise in smaller river systems and may vary for different categories of fish: rates may

A FIXED NET ON A BEACH AWAITS A RISING TIDE AND THE ARRIVAL OF SALMON SWIMMING CLOSE TO THE SURF.

be above 30% for spring-run fish. But overall, angling is a relatively inefficient way to harvest the fish in a sustainable, yet productive fashion, if that indeed is to be the management aim for salmon stocks. The root of the antagonism between netsmen and anglers may well be that the two bodies have quite different understandings of what the management aim is, and, though using the same words, talk quite a different language from one another. This wholly negative conflict could be avoided by the creation of properly structured management plans for each river, but the fragmented nature of salmon fishing ownership – coupled to a lack of data on the salmon population sizes – makes this virtually impossible.

C O N C E R N S   F O R   T H E   F U T U R E

Undoubtedly, the salmon will continue to cause interest, controversy, and passionate argument for as long as we let them swim down to the sea and back again. Each country in Europe has its own set of societies dedicated to ensuring that this is just what will continue to happen. On the international scene the North Atlantic Salmon Conservation Organisation (NASCO) has been trying to regulate the exploitation of salmon in the open sea. Following a treaty signed in 1982, all countries with Atlantic coastlines and a serious interest in the fish participate in discussions about the size of catches allowed in both the Greenland and Faroese fisheries. The scale of the catches has been difficult to negotiate, and with a combined annual quota of 1440 tonnes, there is a large body of anglers on both sides of the Atlantic who would love to see these fisheries closed. As many as 400,000 fish may be landed each year which would otherwise be heading for the rivers and hence the anglers. Hard cash, however, along with depressed fish prices caused by farmed salmon, look like succeeding where patient inter-government negotiations have failed: just as coastal netting stations around Britain have been bought out and shut down by angling interests, international efforts by wealthy sportsmen to buy out the last Faroese long-liners have the same aim.

On a more local scale, interested groups of anglers and owners of salmon waters have formed small societies, clubs, and charitable trusts, all aimed at improving the waters they fish. Many anglers simply want to see more fish in the river so they can get more fish on the bank, so the efforts of many such groups never get further than improving access to the river or the improvement of the river bed for fishing a pool. Useful as this is, it does nothing to advance the stocks of the fish.

Stocking with eggs or fry is most people's idea of the best way to improve the numbers of salmon in a river. But the world is littered with unsuccessful attempts to resurrect lost salmon runs in this manner. First, the genetic quality of the fish stocked must be of local origin. Secondly, the mortality of stocked material is often very high, through competition with other fish or a lack of suitable habitat.

The more enlightened have understood the value of trying to improve the river habitat in order to produce more juveniles. This clearly would benefit the angler as well as safeguarding the salmon's population—there is no point in stocking a river if the habitat is unsuitable or polluted. The Elorn river in Brittany is one of the best examples of this approach. Pollution and blocking of waterways with unnecessary dams were major problems which have been tackled by the initiative of a local group, *l'Association pour la promotion et la protection des saumons en Bretagne*. In Scotland, too, the West Galloway Fisheries Trust is facing habitat degradation problems caused by acidification and silting of the spawning tributaries in the rivers that it looks after. In both cases, it is by attending to the needs of the young salmon in the river that the future of the fish will be assured. But these examples of management are very much exceptions to the rule. Most rivers throughout Europe have very little detailed biological management of their habitat and salmon stocks, and the rivers are left pretty much to look after themselves.

THE NEED FOR PROTECTION

Nowadays, perhaps even more than in the past, salmon stocks need protection. Surely the sheer enthusiasm of so many admirers, coupled with appropriate legislation, should be able to ensure the future of the fish within its present distribution.

A MULTIFILAMENT DRIFT NET IS LOADED ABOARD A DANISH SALMON BOAT IN THE BALTIC. LARGE NUMBERS OF SALMON ARE STILL CAUGHT AT SEA, BUT POLITICAL PRESSURE FROM THE ANGLING COMMUNITY IS MOUNTING TO END THIS 'INDISCRIMINATE' EXPLOITATION.

Farming

Considering the mystique and powerful nomadic habits of the fish, it sounds like sacrilege to factory farm the Atlantic salmon. To confine such a wanderer may well go against many people's sentiments, yet the cage-rearing of salmon has been a phenomenally fast-growing business within the last twenty years, one that is vastly important to rural areas in Norway, Scotland, and Ireland. The industry has attracted more than its share of controversy as environmental issues continue to be raised, and it may also prove to be one of the most important factors affecting the fate of wild stocks. Yet it has a strong fascination and appeal for many people, due in part to the nature of the beast being farmed.

Broodfish and Breeding

Anyone who visits Scotland's or Norway's west coasts cannot fail to see the cages in the sea lochs or fjords, but few will notice the much smaller and compact smolt-producing units on land, where the freshwater part of the life-cycle takes place. Each of these hatcheries may produce up to 1,000,000 smolts, and with roughly 500 smolts giving one tonne of harvested salmon, one hatchery can supply a good-sized farm. Most of the farms keep their own broodstock fish in the sea, right up to or just before spawning time. These fish may weigh 20 lbs or more, and are normally multi-seawinter fish that have shown late maturation and good growth characteristics.

To the farmer, the 'grilsing' habit of maturing after just one winter in the sea is bad news. Prices are lower for these fish in the summer months, when they must be harvested before their flesh deteriorates like that of their wild cousins. As the grilsing rate is in part a genetically-controlled trait, farmers like to use fish that are multi-seawinter for broodstock. By working on selective breeding programmes, individual farming companies have brought their grilsing rates down from more than 50% of their stock maturing after their first winter to less than 20%. Recently, it has been found that high rates of feeding in February and March will encourage fish to mature later that same year, a good example of the environment affecting a fish's 'decision-making'. Surely the same could hold true for wild fish?

By operating a nationwide selective breeding programme, Norwegian government scientists claim to have improved the growth rates of their stocks by up to 15% for each generation over the last ten years. Other countries have not operated such co-ordinated programmes, with the result that Norwegian-farmed fish are considerably heavier at harvesting, on average, than their Scottish and Irish counterparts. The overall effect, important for conservation purposes, is that the farmed salmon in some stocks are many generations removed from their wild ancestors, and so are fast becoming domesticated. Parr with a farmed-fish parentage take fright less easily than parr of wild parentage during normal hatchery operations, such as tank cleaning. Thus the farmed fish is quickly becoming a rather domesticated version of the wild salmon.

Hatching the Eggs

In November the broodfish are stripped manually of their eggs and milt. Producing about 800 eggs per pound of body weight, a large hen fish can be worth a fair amount of money, as the eggs can be worth up to £30 per thousand or more. The eggs are fertilised by mixing them with milt in a bowl. The fertilised eggs are then placed in their thousands in the incubation system of the hatchery. Various methods are used, from racks of perforated trays to hatchery bins where the eggs are left in a great mass, with filtered and sterilised water flowing up through them. Such systems may get a regular dose of an antifungal agent to keep the fluffy white Saprolegnia fungus from

FARMED OR WILD, SALMON ARE GRACEFUL FISH.

Smolt—rearing cages in a Scottish freshwater loch. To avoid enriching the loch with phosphorus — a common element in fish feed and one that normally limits the growth rate of aquatic plants — the Water Purification Boards restrict farmers in the amount of food they can give to the fish.

overgrowing healthy eggs. Here the eggs will sit until they are close to hatching, when they will be moved to hatching troughs, which are long, shallow tanks where the farmer tries to mimic the quiet, dark environment of the redd.

Following hatching, when the yolk sac is almost used up, and at an equivalent stage to when their wild counterparts are pushing up through the gravel redds, the alevins will be moved to large circular tanks. Here the crucial first feeding takes place. An energy-rich pellet feed, appearing more like dust than anything else, is offered first to start a life of steady feeding and, the farmer hopes, steady growth.

The Feed

Throughout its life the fish is fed on a high-protein diet consisting mainly of a fish-meal component, though partial substitutions with soya bean and single-cell proteins have been tried with considerable success. The farmed salmon could be considered simply as a vehicle to upgrade fish protein from low to high-quality form! Compared with conventional agricultural factory-farming, the salmon-farming industry is a much smaller user of industrial fish resources, i.e. fish-meal produced from species which are not used for human consumption. It would be ironic if pressures on industrial fish stocks – sand-eel, capelin, or menhaden – taken in part to feed salmon in cages, were to affect the feeding and survival of wild fish in the sea, as some people now claim.

In their shoals of thousands, the young parr are given an easy supply of feed, either by hand or by automatic feeder. After first feeding they may be moved from their tanks to net cages if the farmer is operating in a loch as many farms now do. Here the natural territorial behaviour is subdued by the sheer numbers of fish. Holding a feeding station in a shoal, individuals will dart from their place to seize a pellet, then turn, flashing their yellowish bellies at the surface.

Work on a smolt farm consists of a solid mix of feeding and grading the slow from the fast growers. Potential disaster is never far away and always seems to happen in the middle of the night or at weekends when pipes freeze or pumps fail and inlets become blocked.

THE SMOLT

At the end of its first year, in April or May, the parr will reach a body weight of at least two or three ounces and, like the wild fish, will go through the smolt transformation as it prepares for a life at sea. Here though, it is the farmer who decides when and if the fish goes to sea. For a few weeks the fish is in perfect readiness for a direct transfer to sea water, and if the farmer miscues this timing he can seriously affect the smolt's subsequent growth. Those fish that are not quite ready will become runts in their salt water cage. Putting all their energies into salt and water balance, they soon take on a tadpole appearance as they slowly starve. They can live for months after the transfer to sea water, but they will be a fraction of the size of those ready for the move.

The smolt farmer aims to produce all his smolts in just one year, and may push about 80% of his stock into smolting in this time. Some of the larger companies use heated water to accelerate the growth rates and produce smolts in less than a year. Whatever the method, for every two or three eggs incubated the previous autumn the farmer will normally produce one smolt at the end of the year.

With sea cages often in remote places, getting his smolts to the sea farms can be difficult for the farmer. The modern smolt, instead of swimming to the sea, travels by air, sea, or road. Kept in specially-oxygenated transporting tanks, the smolts may be moved from one end of the country to the other by truck. Some operators sling such tanks or buckets under a helicopter, while others use specially-constructed well boats to deliver the fish by sea.

FARMING THE SEA

With the smolt in the sea, the farmer and his bank manager breathe a sigh of relief, if that is where their responsibility ends. Those concerned with ongrowing the stock in sea cages have a nervous year or two before their stock is ready for market. The dangers of disease, storm, seal, and theft are never far from their minds. As with any beast that

A VARIATION ON THE STAG'S HEAD – A NORWEGIAN FISH FARMER HOLDS THE TROPHY HEAD OF A 33KG
BROODSTOCK COCK FISH.

A FISH EYE'S VIEW OF A SALMON LOUSE, IN THIS INSTANCE A FRESHWATER SPECIES ARGULUS. SUCH PARASITES CAUSE GREAT ECONOMIC LOSSES TO FARMERS, WHO USE PESTICIDES DEVELOPED FOR AGRICULTURAL AND DOMESTIC USE TO CONTROL THEM. SCIENTISTS ARE CURRENTLY RESEARCHING ALTERNATIVE THERAPIES, FROM VACCINES TO ONIONS!

is kept in high densities in unnatural conditions, the risk of disease is high, and transmission can be rapid. There are several microbial agents that cause continual losses, and a great deal of research has been carried out into studying, identifying, and looking for cures for these diseases. Losses can be spectacular, but normally there is a continual trickle of mortalities which are a constant drain on a farmer's financial plans. The most problematic of the more common bacterial diseases – furunculosis – normally requires antibiotic treatment. More than eyebrows have been raised as to the amounts of antibiotics – measured in tonnes in the Norwegian industry – that are released into the environment each year, though all is under strict veterinary control and no fish are allowed onto the market following a treatment. Antibiotic resistance is a widespread and nagging worry. Farmers are having to tighten up on their use of such drugs and are looking for more natural ways to control the causative organisms. Throughout the industry, farmers are now realising the value of a less intensive and more environmentally-sensitive approach to growing their fish, as a fish in a polluted environment will be a stressed animal, and stressed animals are invariably more susceptible to disease.

Not all the pests of salmon are as small as viruses or bacteria, and one parasite that needs continual checking is a crustacean, the sea louse. Grazing on the mucus, skin and blood of the fish, the sea lice remove the salmon's natural protective covering and soon open up sores which can lead to secondary infections. Sea lice infest wild salmon, and an angler seeing them on his catch knows that his fish is a fresh-run animal from the sea, as lice will normally drop off their host after twenty-four to forty-eight hours in fresh water. The farmer is less happy to spot them, and he uses various organophosphate pesticides – Nuvan and Aquagard have been recent brand-names – to keep them under check, which causes concern amongst some environmentalists. Toxic to sea lice, these pesticides are also very toxic to other forms of marine life. However, being quickly broken down and diluted through the sea, their deleterious effects are possibly only seen close to the treated cages.

POLLUTION CONCERNS

The use of pesticides to control the lice has many drawbacks. To start with, there is rather naturally a degree of consumer resistance to their use. Secondly, they are toxic to the fish. A third major problem is that they only kill the older stages of the louse – juveniles are unaffected. So farmers are keen to find more natural ways to control these parasites.

A FEMALE
SEALOUSE
LEPEOPHTHEIRUS
SALMONIS

Recently, scientists in Norway have experimented with various species of a small coastal fish, the wrasse, which will pick and eat the lice off the heads and backs of salmon in a cage, reducing the need to use chemical treatments. These fish are now widely used throughout the Scottish, Irish, and Norwegian industries, and this example of biological control shows how potential pollution problems can be reduced with a little ingenuity. Indeed, some farmers have gone beyond the bounds of ingenuity into the realms of the seemingly ridiculous, using onion and garlic concentrates in the salmon feed to keep the lice away – although this is yet to be a proven delousing technique under scientifically controlled experimental conditions.

Other nuisances to the farmer include the same predators which prey upon the wild fish: seals, cormorants, and herons. Fish-farmers have come under what has been (at least partially) justified criticism of needless culling of these animals, for which shooting licences are granted. Young herons in particular are likely to be peppered with shot, as they lack the natural caution of the surviving adults. Seals do cause serious problems from time to time, and anti-predator nets hung outside the cages can keep some of their unwelcome attention away. Recently, sonic scares which imitate attacking killer whales have been used to some effect, though the seals will soon ignore these, to their own detriment if a real whale happens by. Random sound generators are now widely used, disturbing the would-be attacking seal and forcing it to seek a quieter meal. Again, with a little thought, such measures can reduce problems in a more peaceful and acceptable fashion than the use of the bullet.

The environmental lobby is also concerned with the visual impact of the sea cages, though cage sites are more transient and less drastic in terms of impact than some modern farming and forestry practices. Rather understandably, such arguments wear a bit thin with those charged with developing the economy of rural regions, as the criticism normally comes from people living outside the fish-farming areas. The pollution from fish farms is potentially more serious. This can be a problem on freshwater sites, and anyone who has watched marsh gas bubbling from sediments downstream from smolt units, or white sulphur-reducing bacterial mats covering formerly clean upland streams and lochs, has to admit that such smolt units can harm the environment. Today, the authorities responsible for water pollution control treat freshwater farms as they would any other industry and control the amount of polluting nutrients that any particular farm is allowed to release into the water.

Despite the potentially greater impact of freshwater farms on their environment, public attention has focused more on the pollution from farming sites at sea. This concern about the marine side of the farming operation has probably been triggered by the quite unconnected but very well publicised blooms of algae in the North Sea and on the west coast of Britain, along with the very obvious deterioration in the health of our seas. However, the enriching effects of marine farms are actually only seen close to cages, and sites left fallow may recover to their original state within a few years. If only the same could be said for modern agricultural practices.

WORKING THE FARM

The work on sea cages is hard and often tedious. Feeding is a constant routine, and lifting and changing nets is extremely heavy work, unless winches are used. A net that has been left in the sea too long in the summer will weigh more than a tonne, thanks to millions of barnacles and mussels that gleefully settle on the mesh. The slimy tentacles of the red jellyfish add an extra stinging hardship. Not surprisingly, there is sometimes a high turnover of staff on farms.

SEA CAGES IN LOCH EINORT, SKYE. A LARGE FARM LIKE THIS MAY EMPLOY TWENTY OR MORE PEOPLE IN AN AREA THAT HAS LITTLE OTHER EMPLOYMENT PROSPECTS.

At sea the scope for disaster is even greater than in the smolt farms, with cages being washed from their moorings, and worse. In one spectacular case on the west coast of Scotland, a Bulgarian factory ship was blown through a group of cages in a storm, creating a bonanza for local fishermen. But to liven up the tedium of work, life can be quite wild, with limitless scope for 'high jinks' – bothy life of a sort is still very much alive in such places.

The Harvest

The culmination of the farming process is the harvest, when fish are stunned with the traditional club or 'priest', before being packed in ice. Alternatively, they are anaesthetised with carbon dioxide, bled, and sent for smoking. At least half the farmed-salmon output goes for smoking now, though unlike its Pacific counterpart of John West fame, none is used for canning. By 1982 world farmed-salmon production had overtaken the harvest of 9800 tonnes of wild fish, and by 1985 there was a threefold difference between the two. Norway is the major producer, followed by Scotland, the Faroes, Ireland, Iceland, Canada, Chile, and Tasmania. The huge output from farms has meant that Atlantic salmon have lost their luxury image in many markets and now have to compete with the more down market Pacific salmon, of which the wild catch is reckoned to be over 600,000 tonnes per year. Farmed production of salmon throughout the world

was rising towards 300,000 tonnes per year by 1991, with Pacific salmon forming only a small fraction of this total. However, it now seems likely that production will stabilise at a figure closer to 200,000 tonnes per year. As production soared, the price of salmon dropped quite dramatically in real terms throughout the 80s, and now many farms are in serious financial difficulties as the selling price has fallen below the cost of production. Norwegian farmers, in particular, are in trouble. An inadequate system of controlling production, and subsequently

FEEDING IS NORMALLY DONE BY HAND AND AUTOMATIC FEED DISPENSERS. CAREFUL FEEDING AND THE USE OF HIGH QUALITY DIETS, EASILY DIGESTED BY THE FISH, CAN REDUCE THE AMOUNT OF ENRICHING NUTRIENTS RELEASED INTO THE SEA, AND HENCE THE POLLUTION FROM SUCH CAGES.

sales, led to accusations of 'dumping' of cheap salmon on the American and European markets. The former have slapped huge tariffs on Norwegian imports, and Scottish and Irish farmers have done their best to get EC action against the Norwegians. Add to this a crisis in the Norwegian banks, who have been over-generous in their loans to farmers, and the news headlines of 'crisis in salmon farming' are quite understandable.

THE EFFECT ON WILD FISH

The drop in prices for salmon has had a huge effect on the wild netting industry. A poorer price for their fish in the face of competition from farmed material means that wild fishery companies have shown less resilience than they might have done previously to bodies such as the Atlantic Salmon Conservation Trust, who have bought out and closed down many such businesses. The rise of the farming industry and the accompanying decline of the netting industry is just one of the effects that salmon farming has had on wild fish. Another is the effect that escaped farmed fish may have on the genetic purity of wild stocks, a possibility which is currently the subject of considerable interest, and one that arouses very strong emotions.

It is only recently that biochemical measurements of the genetic make-up of farmed and wild fish have been made. Depending on which study and which scientist you pay attention to, there has been some degree of loss of genetic variability in farmed stocks compared with wild fish. However, scientists have inspected only a tiny fraction of the estimated 10,000 to 100,000 genes in the salmon, and no-one understands the

THE FINAL HARVEST — BUT HOW DIFFERENT FROM WILD FISH? THE FLESH QUALITY CAN BE EVEN BETTER THAN THAT OF WILD FISH UNDER CERTAIN CONDITIONS, IF THE FARMER HAS DONE HIS JOB PROPERLY — BUT IT CAN ALSO BE WORSE. QUALITY CONTROL IS NOW THE NAME OF THE FARMERS' GAME.

functional significance of the variation (or lack of it) in the genes examined. For those genes studied, however, farmed fish are now different from wild ones in terms of their genetic variability, even when they originate from the same river source.

Many aspects of the wild fish's behaviour, physiology, and form have a demonstrable genetic control, including the ability to migrate successfully back to the home river and resistance to disease. These varying characteristics have their origins in the animals' variable genetic make-up, and so the intrusion of 'foreign' genetic material into a population must certainly have some effect, though whether this is necessarily an adverse one would depend on the particular circumstances.

Farmed fish do escape, they do run up rivers, and they can spawn with wild fish. Whether this will have a measurable effect on the wild population's genetic make-up will depend on the number of escaped fish in relation to the number of wild fish present in a river. If the ratio is no greater than that normally found with wild fish straying from other rivers, then it is unlikely that any great influence of the escaped fish will be registered. Where the numbers of escaped farmed fish are high in relation to the wild fish, then a considerable shift in genetic patterns might be expected. Whether or not this would then be detrimental to the wild population is impossible to say with our current knowledge, but a loss of biological 'fitness' is theoretically possible.

The 'genetic pollution' controversy seems set to run for many years. This kind of controversy is not new in Norway, where salmon-farming research scientists have been inadvertently responsible for the loss of wild salmon from at least thirty rivers by introducing to the waters a parasite, Gyrodactylus, through infected fish imported from Sweden. The Norwegian fish lacked the natural resilience to this parasite that the native Swedish fish had, and whole stocks were lost as a result. It is a good demonstration of how wild stocks can vary from one area to another, and the unexpected impact that farmed fish can have on wild stocks.

Partly because of the Gyrodactylus problem, famers are now being accused of spreading 'disease' via escaped fish, and infecting wild fish in rivers. Furunculosis is the main worry, but in the British Isles this disease was endemic in wild salmonids before the start of farming. It was introduced into Norwegian waters via infected farmed stock, but it is uncertain whether it has had any real effect on wild populations there. In most situations disease only affects stressed fish. Wild salmon have long been the victims of disease, as the process of maturation inadvertently lowers their resistance to infectious bugs. The most infamous disease of wild fish, ulcerative dermal necrosis, or UDN, has never had a causative organism identified and, though always affecting wild fish to some degree, has never been seen in farmed fish.

A great deal of the criticism aimed at salmon faming in connection with its supposed impact on wild fish and the environment has been at best unfair and at times completely mischievous. An example is the blame that has been attached to salmon farms, particularly in Ireland, for the disappearance of sea-trout from many famous angling waters. The supposed cause are the sea lice emanating from salmon cages, but the accusers have conveniently ignored the fact that this decline also involves rivers far removed from salmon-farming areas. A more widespread cause is at work, though no-one is sure where the root of the problem lies. However, sea lice from farms could be a contributory cause in certain areas, and a wise precaution is not to site farms close to the mouths of salmon and sea trout rivers, a step that the Norwegians have already taken, though for reasons of limiting the impact of escaped fish rather than for fear of sealice.

RANCHING

Farmers, particularly in Iceland, are now 'ranching' salmon, i.e. growing the smolts in a normal farm then releasing these fish into the sea and utilising their homing instincts to catch them on their return migration, ready-fed and grown with a minimum of effort. It sounds perfect, but the return rates obviously need to be satisfactory to cover the costs of producing the smolts. Only in Iceland, where sea netting is banned, does this approach currently make sense. In other European waters, where public fishing rights exist, interception of the rancher's fish by others is too great a risk to make this a sensible business option. But the idea of ranching is surely one of the best ways to harvest the sea's great riches in a predictable fashion. Ranchers argue that their fish is a prime one, superior in quality to the normal farmed beast, something that fish-farmers have strenuously denied in the past.

FARMED OR WILD?

Even in death, then, the salmon causes controversy and discussion. Can *you* tell the difference between a farmed and a wild fish? That question has been asked a million times, and as many say yes as say no. As a whole fish, the farmed animal certainly looks different, as its fins are worn and stunted compared with those of the wild fish, and farmed fish usually have a higher body fat content than wild ones. After cooking, it becomes more difficult to distinguish one from the other. Top-class chefs are certainly happy enough with the farmed product, and processors prefer the uniformity and predictability of supply that the farmer can give. Some folk turn up their noses at farmed fish in preference to wild, but given two unlabelled pieces of the two kinds, how many people could spot the difference? The reality is that the farmed fish can be a top-class product in its own right, and a healthy dish to boot.

whose devotion to tasting duties in the pursuit of knowledge obviously deserves a medal!

In the frozen conditions of cold storage, slow oxidation occurs of those all important long-chain fatty acids which are so good for our health. It is this oxidation that gives rise to the chemicals responsible for 'off flavour'. In this respect salmon again fares better than marine fish, as the highly-unsaturated fatty acids are apparently protected by layers of triglyceride fats in the connective tissue, so reducing the oxidation rate and the development of off flavour. Nevertheless, keeping salmon frozen for many months will eventually lead to this problem.

The pH of fish flesh is vital in affecting the texture of the flesh. After death, some glycogen breaks down to lactic acid, causing a drop in the pH which then gives the flesh a tough texture. In farmed salmon in mid-summer there appears to be a natural pH drop from the normal 6.5 to 6.1; this will affect texture. The one compensation is that at lower pH values the spoilage from bacterial activity is reduced. Otherwise, with the exception of spawning fish, the pH is constant through the year.

All in all, one dead fish is not necessarily the same as another: maturation sees to that. To avoid the sweet-flavoured inosine monophosphate turning to the bitter hypoxanthine compound, the newly-killed fish must be kept as cool as possible. Freeze, but not for too long. Three months is a good rule of thumb.

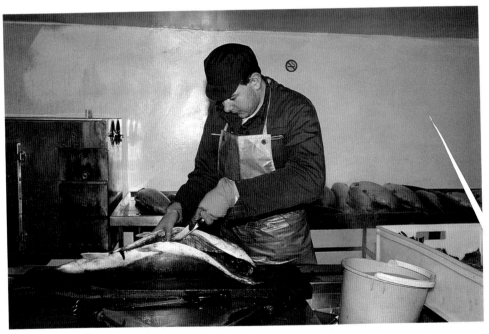

THE BACKBONE IS REMOVED BEFORE SALTING AND SMOKING. A HIGH CLASS DISH IN THE MAKING.

POSTSCRIPT: WHERE TO FISH

It is possible — with a little forward planning — to fish on the various rivers mentioned in this text, and the prices need not be exorbitant. The following notes and addresses will serve as an introduction.

SPAIN

There is a two-tier licence system. First, a general licence from the local government (*xunta*) allows the angler to catch salmon and trout in all free areas (*zonas libras*) — not surprisingly the waters where such fish are rarities — but not on the protected beats (the *cotos*) for which additional permits are granted on a ballot basis. Applications to this ballot normally have to be made nine months in advance, but this varies from region to region. The best months for salmon are from March to May, but the season extends to the end of June or July, according to the region. The tourist office produce leaflets on where to fish, but extra information on the Rio Deva and the other Cantabrian rivers is available from: *Servicio de Montes, Caza y Conservacion de la Naturaleza, Calle Rodriques, 5, 1, 39071 Santander, Spain.* For the Rio Cares and the Asturias rivers, write to: *Servicio de Conservacion de la Naturaleza, Calle Uria, 10-1, 33003 Oviedo, Spain.* For more information on the Gallician streams, try: *Consejeria de Agricultura, Pesca y Alimentacion, Carretera de Santiago a Lugo, San Lazaro, Santiago de Compostela, Spain.*

FRANCE

Fishing is not expensive in France, and day tickets can be bought from any local tackle shop. For the Gave d'Oloron, the best water lies between Navarrenx and St Marie d'Oloron, and tickets can be bought in these two towns. May is the best month, but the season extends to the end of July. For the Allier, Moulins, near Vichy, is the place to go, the season stretching from end of April to the middle of July. The Elorn season ends in mid-July, the last month having a fly-only rule. Permits to fish the Elorn can be bought from the tackle shop in Landerneau or the river interpretation centre in Sizun. More information can be sought from the local angling improvement society: *AAPP Elorn, 4 Oree du Bois, 29800 La Martyre, Bretagne, France.*

GREAT BRITAIN

For the whole of the UK, the local tackle shop is often the best source of tickets for any particular water. Estate agents will also handle ticket sales, and information can be sought from the local tourist office. However, much of the best water is booked years in advance, and waiting lists are long. Even then, the angler may be without a chance. Do not hope to buy a ticket on the River Laxford in Sutherland — probably one of the best salmon rivers in the world — unless you have the correct connections in high society. However, it is possible to get on to other famous waters. On the Tay system, day tickets for various parts of the river can be bought. Try in May/June or September/October. The Perth tackle shop, P D Malloch (tel. 0738 32316) can supply tickets for different beats, sometimes at short notice. For ticket details on the whole river, contact: *Perthshire Tourist Board, 45 High Street, Perth PH1 5TJ* (Or tel. 0738 38353). On the Tweed system, where most fish run in September and October, a telephone hotline service will give you access at short notice: 0898 666412.

IRELAND

As in the UK, local tackle shops and hotels are the best source of information and tickets. The local tourist offices will also help. For the Moy, where the season runs from the beginning of February to the mid-October, tickets can be bought in Ballina. For initial information try contacting: *Moy Fishery Office, Ridge Pool Road, Ballina, County Mayo, Ireland.* (Or tel. 096 21332)

It is often necessary to book well in advance in order to secure a place on any of the better known rivers in all of the Scandic countries. Again, the tourist information offices or, in the case of Iceland, the airline Icelandair, will supply information. For the smaller rivers, tackle shops or hotels can supply tickets at short notice — sometimes! To fish in Norway for salmon or trout one first needs a national permit, covering a season, that can be bought in any post office. For the Alta, where the main fish run is in late summer, for information contact: *Alta Laksefiskeri I/S, 9510 Elvebakken, Finnmark, Iceland.* For the Tana, where the more casual angler has a good chance of obtaining a permit at short notice, contact for advance information: *Fylkesmannen i Finnmark, Miljovernavdelingen, Damsveien 1, 9800 Vadso, Finnmark, Norway.*

For those on the western side of the North Atlantic, there is no shortage of opportunity to catch Atlantic salmon. For those keen to try, here are some starting points.

UNITED STATES

One non-migratory form, the sebago salmon, is found in many of the lakes of New York, Maine, Vermont and New Hampshire. Maine is perhaps the best state for this fish, with Moosehead Lake, Eagle Lake, and Sebago Lake being well worth a visit. Permits are readily available for the casual visitor and are not expensive. April or May, after the ice breaks up, is the time to go after these small but hard-fighting fish.

CANADA

There are numerous lakes in Labrador, New Brunswick, Newfoundland, Nova Scotia, Ontario and Quebec where the casual angler can get easy access to land-locked salmon populations. As well as the common sebago form in the lakes, there is another type, the ouananiche, which lives in the fast-flowing waters of the Upper Sanguenay in Quebec. For those who want to try for the normal migratory form, the maritime provinces are blessed with numerous rivers. It is very hard to get on to much of the good water, as beats are run by private clubs and prices are high. But there are numerous private and state-run angling waters where one can get a ticket. For the world famous Miramichi river in New Brunswick, try contacting:

Department of Tourism, PO Box 12345, Fredericton, New Brunswick E3B 5C3.

Only fly-fishing is allowed, a state permit is a necessity, and a local permit will be required on most waters.

Glossary and Origins of Names

ALEVIN a newly-hatched young salmon which still has its yolk sac and is resident in the redd. The name is French in origin, '*alevain*', from the verb 'to raise'.

BAGGOT an adult female salmon that has failed to spawn and returns to the sea full of eggs. The name, derived from the Scots 'baggit', initially referred to any animal full of spawn.

FRY a young salmon emerging from the redd and ready to start feeding

GRILSE an adult salmon returning to the river after only one winter at sea. The name first appears in early English documents, with many different spellings, from 'gilse' to 'grissel'. It is probably derived from the Scandinavian '*gra laks*' (grey salmon) or the French '*gris*' (grey); the French now use the word *castillon* for this stage.

JACK SALMON a salmon that matures early, either as a parr or else in its first autumn at sea, i.e. in the same year as it entered sea water as a smolt. 'Jack' is a common prefix to denote a small or young specimen of an animal.

KELT a salmon that has spawned and is returning to the sea. The name is English in origin.

KIPPER a mature male salmon in its spawning colours. An English word, its usage for salmon predates the more usual herring use and has the same derivation as 'kype'.

KYPE the hooked lower jaw of a mature male salmon. The word was used in a more general sense in Scots and English to describe such a facial feature. It has its root in the German word '*Kippe*' (a point, peak, or tip).

PARR a young salmon in the river that has developed the characteristic grey-blue 'thumbprint' marks down its flanks. The name first appears in Scottish documents, but its origin is unknown. The French equivalent is '*tacon*' and the Spanish '*pinto*'.

PRIEST the club, usually wooden, used for killing salmon by a blow to the head. The origin needs no explanation!

REDD the nest dug by a female fish in the gravel of a stream bed, in which her eggs are laid. It may be derived from the Scots verb 'to redd', i.e. to clean or sweep, effectively describing the hen fish's actions when digging the redd or else the clean appearance of the gravel after the redd is dug.

SMOLT a silver-coloured migratory juvenile salmon that leaves the river in spring or early summer. Scots in origin, the name is now widely used through Europe.

FURTHER READING

A book like this is drawn from a wide variety of sources. Most of these are research papers published in the scientific press; these primary sources are usually inaccessible to the general reader as the relevant journals are not carried in public libraries. For the reader who wishes to explore the subject further, the following books give a more detailed account of the salmon than is possible here.

Buckland, John and Arthur Oglesby. *A Guide to Salmon Flies*. Marlborough: Crowwood Press, 1990.

Drummond Sedgewick, Stephen. *The Salmon Handbook*. London: Andre Deutsch, 1982.

Falkus, Hugh. *Salmon Fishing*. London: Witherby, 1984.

Laird, L. and E. Needham, eds. *Salmon and Trout Farming*. Chichester: Ellis Horwood Ltd, 1989

Little, Crawford. *The Great Salmon Beats*. Newton Abbot and London: David and Charles, 1989.

Maitland, P. S. and R. N. Campbell. *Freshwater Fishes of the British Isles*. London: Harper Collins, 1992.

Mills, D. H. *Ecology and Management of Atlantic Salmon*. London: Chapman and Hall, 1989.

Netboy, Anthony. *The Salmon: Their Fight for Survival*. Boston: Houghton Mifflin Co, 1974.

Oglesby, Arthur. *Fly Fishing for Salmon and Sea Trout*. London: Crowwood Press, 1986.

O'Reilly, Peter. *Trout and Salmon Rivers of Ireland — An Angler's Guide*. London: Merlin Unwin, 1991.

Rosenthal, Mike. *North America's Freshwater Fishing Book*. New York: Scribner, 1984.

Shearer, W. M. *The Atlantic Salmon: Natural History, Exploitation, and Future Management*. Oxford: Fishing News Books, Blackwells Scientific Press, 1992.

Swainbank, Todd and Eric Seidler. *Taking Freshwater Game Fish*. Woodstock, Vermont: The Countryman Press, 1984.

Wolff, Lee. *The Atlantic Salmon*. New York: Nick Lyons Books, 1986.

In addition to these, anyone interested in salmon conservation can contact the Atlantic Salmon Trust, an organisation which promotes salmon conservation and publishes short reviews on various aspects of salmon management. Their address is *The Atlantic Salmon Trust, Moulin, Pitlochry, Perthshire PH16 5JQ, Scotland.*